"Beautifully written . . . Smith should be just as celebrated for her prose."

—*Town & Country*

"Incredibly relatable . . . At turns devastating and darkly funny."

—*Columbus Monthly*

"*You Could Make This Place Beautiful* is about recognizing your own worth in your relationship, and in the world."

—*Slate*

"A poet's memoir . . . [Smith] has an uncanny ability to boil down giant ideas into tiny, dense sentences that are both playful and heartbreaking."

—*Shondaland*

"An anatomy of . . . an artist stepping into her own light, of a mother working out how to create a loving family on her own."

—*Bomb*

"Smith's prose is as warm and welcoming as her poetry."

—*Chicago Review of Books*

"Smith opens her heart like a book, dog-earing moments both painful and joyous. . . . Smith's conjuring of beauty through pain and her special blend of vulnerability and encouragement go down like a healing tonic."

—*Booklist* (starred review)

"*You Could Make This Place Beautiful* is a sparklingly brilliant memoir-in-vignettes that only Maggie Smith could write. Yet this is a book for everyone—who among us has never had our world upended by the loss of a relationship? Maggie Smith's powerful mastery of language, and amazing ability to portray life in all its rich messiness, is on full display in this bold, brutally candid, and yes, beautiful, book."

—Isaac Fitzgerald, *New York Times* bestselling author of *Dirtbag, Massachusetts*

"In this lightning bolt of a debut memoir, Maggie Smith gives us the truth of healing in form as much as story: getting through is no pretty, linear narrative. It's one chapter forward and five chapters back. *You Could Make This Place Beautiful* gave me back a part of myself I thought was gone for good: the knowledge that beauty isn't something out there to find. It's in us."

—Megan Stielstra, author of *The Wrong Way to Save Your Life*

"Listen, you may not need me to tell you what you already know about the shining star that is Maggie Smith, but you can certainly add me to the chorus of those singing her praises about *You Could Make This Place Beautiful*. Among her singular gifts as a writer are the way she swiftly brings her poetry to her prose; her willingness to show up to the page with aspirational levels of vulnerability, grace, and joy; and a clarity of heart amid the heartbreak that together makes this a moving and gorgeous must-read."

—Elizabeth Crane, author of *This Story Will Change*

"When personal tragedy strikes us, first we have to survive, then we have to begin healing. This exquisite book will help you do both. Reading Smith's memoir, I laughed and gasped and ugly-cried and somehow began to process ten years of my own pent-up, frozen grief. This book is nothing less than a cathartic miracle."

—Alissa Nutting, author of *Made for Love*

ONE SIGNAL
PUBLISHERS

ATRIA

ALSO BY MAGGIE SMITH

My Thoughts Have Wings

Goldenrod

Keep Moving: The Journal

Keep Moving: Notes on Loss, Creativity, and Change

Good Bones

The Well Speaks of Its Own Poison

Lamp of the Body

You Could
Make This Place
Beautiful

A MEMOIR

Maggie Smith

ONE SIGNAL
PUBLISHERS
—
ATRIA
NEW YORK • LONDON • TORONTO • SYDNEY • NEW DELHI

ONE SIGNAL
PUBLISHERS

ATRIA

An Imprint of Simon & Schuster, LLC
1230 Avenue of the Americas
New York, NY 10020

Copyright © 2023 by Maggie Smith

First One Signal Publishers/Atria Paperback edition June 2024

ONE SIGNAL PUBLISHERS / ATRIA PAPERBACK and colophon are
trademarks of Simon & Schuster, LLC

Simon & Schuster: Celebrating 100 Years of Publishing in 2024

For information about special discounts for bulk purchases,
please contact Simon & Schuster Special Sales at 1-866-506-1949 or
business@simonandschuster.com.

The Simon & Schuster Speakers Bureau can bring authors to your live event. For
more information or to book an event, contact the Simon & Schuster Speakers
Bureau at 1-866-248-3049 or visit our website at www.simonspeakers.com.

Interior design by Dana Sloan

Manufactured in the United States of America

1 3 5 7 9 10 8 6 4 2

Library of Congress Cataloging-in-Publication Data has been applied for.

ISBN 978-1-9821-8585-5
ISBN 978-1-9821-8586-2 (pbk)
ISBN 978-1-9821-8587-9 (ebook)

I am out with lanterns, looking for myself.

—Emily Dickinson

PROLOGUE

Before we go any further together, me with my lanterns, you following close behind, light flickering on both of our faces, I want to be clear about something: This isn't a tell-all. A tell-all would need an omniscient narrator—godlike, hovering over the whole scene, seeing into the houses, listening to the conversations and phone calls, reading the texts and emails. I'm jealous of this all-knowing narrator, even though she doesn't exist. I want to know what she knows.

This isn't a tell-all because "all" is something we can't access. We don't get "all." "Some," yes. "Most" if we're lucky. "All," no. There's no such thing as a tell-all, only a tell-some—a tell-most, maybe. This is a tell-mine, and the *mine* keeps changing, because *I* keep changing. The mine is slippery like that.

This isn't a tell-all because some of what I'm telling you is what I *don't* know. I'm offering the absences, too—the spaces I know aren't empty, but I can't see what's inside them. Like the white spaces between stanzas in a poem: What is unspoken, unwritten there? How do we read those silences?

The book you're holding in your hands was many books before it was this one. Nested inside this version are the others: the version I began deep inside my sadness, thumbed into my phone in bed on sleepless nights; the one I scribbled out with sparks in my hair. You'll see pieces of those books inside this one. Why? Because I'm trying to get to the truth, and I can't get there except by looking at the whole, even the parts I don't want to see. Maybe especially those parts. I've had to move into—and through—the darkness to find the beauty.

Spoiler alert: It's there. The beauty's there.

I know the real people who are part of this story, the story of my life, may read it. Most importantly, my children may read this book someday (hi kids, I love you). I share this story with them because we share the life. But this tell-mine is just that—my experience. There's no such thing as a tell-all because we can only ever speak for ourselves.

Where do I begin? I could begin in my childhood. I could begin in a college classroom where I sat across from the man I would later marry; or in a Denny's on State Route 23, where we wrote private jokes on the sugar packets; or in our first apartment in Grandview, where I was hit by lightning the night we moved in; or in the hospital where my children were born and I was born and my mother was born; or on our last family vacation, when I packed my sadness and took it with us to the beach; or in my lawyer's office, rubbing a small, sharp piece of rose quartz under the conference table; or at the end of everything that was also somehow the beginning; or in this moment, writing to you, watching fog skim the roofs of houses across the street, as if the clouds had grown tired of treading air and had let themselves sink; or, or, or . . .

This story could begin in any of these places. I'm beginning here.

PINECONE

It was an unusual pinecone, the one my husband brought home from a business trip as a souvenir for our five-year-old son, Rhett. *Like a small wooden grenade*, I thought.

My son has always been one to collect what he calls "nature treasures"— pinecones, acorns, stones, flowers, shells. I find them when I empty his pockets, doing the laundry. I find them in my purses and coat pockets, where he's slipped them for me to find.

This pinecone, brought home to Ohio on an airplane, sat on one of our two dining room sideboards. We bought the pair years ago to house our white wedding dishes, the ones we'd registered for, because the serving platters and even the dinner plates were too large for our kitchen cabinets.

The house was built in 1925. It's periwinkle and white—periwinkle just like the crayon, likely an accident of paint that looked gray enough in the can. Built before central air-conditioning, the house has so many windows, and so few walls without them, we had no idea when we bought the house where we would put the couch or hang the large paintings.

There are so many windows, the house is lit naturally all day long, and you can follow the sunlight as it moves from the back of the house at sunrise to the front at sunset. There are so many windows, I couldn't bear to hang blinds or full curtain panels. With only café curtains covering the lower halves of all the windows, my head can be seen floating from room to room at night from the street. There are so many windows, living in this house is like living in a glass display case, especially after dark. There are few places to hide.

A few weeks after my husband returned from his latest business trip, one of a few trips he'd taken to the same city in recent months, something felt off. Something had shifted, maybe just slightly, but perceptibly.

One night he went to bed before me, and I stayed up late writing, sitting on the brown sectional sofa we'd had to float in the middle of the living room. The leather messenger bag he carried to work was sitting in its usual spot on a dining room chair, open, its unbuckled flap hanging over the back of the chair.

Everyone was asleep in the house but me; even the dog, our brindle-and-white Boston terrier, Phoebe, was likely snoring on the couch. I call her "the marble rye" because of the way she looks like a dense loaf of bread when she's curled up.

Everyone was asleep, so no one was watching what I did next, but I felt watched. There are so many windows that someone walking by our house that night could've seen me from the front walk, but that wasn't what made me feel uneasy, nearly seasick, as if I'd just stepped off a boat. It was as if an omniscient narrator—the one I imagine now, the one whose knowledge I envy—was watching me as I set my laptop down and walked over to the chair. I cringe to think of it now—my hand reaching into the bag, rifling through the manila file folders and legal pads inside. I was—*am*—ashamed, yes, for snooping. Though I would be more ashamed if I had found nothing. Nothing was not what I found.

There was a postcard. I saw a woman's name. An address in the city he'd been visiting for work. Her address. I read what he'd written to her. He didn't know what kind of pinecone it was, the one they'd picked up on their walk together.

After I read the postcard and slid it back into the bag where I'd found it, I kept looking. What else was there? I pulled out the blank book he kept in his bag, like the one I carry for jotting down ideas for poems, lists, phone numbers, funny things my kids say.

I flipped to the last entry, the one followed by blank pages. I wanted what I read there—the story of a walk, a woman, a house, her sleeping children upstairs—to be notes for a novel or a play he was working on. But I knew these weren't characters. They were people. I knew this wasn't fiction. It was his life. My life. Ours.

How I picture it: That life—the past, the beforelife, the beforemath—was a boat. I was on it with my husband, and later our daughter joined us, and still later, our son.

The sea was sometimes calm, and we could see right down into the water. We could see everything beneath us. I felt like we were being held—kept afloat, buoyed—by everything we saw. Other times the sea was rough and gray, ruffles on the waves when they curled over and broke.

There are stowaways in so many stories about long journeys across the sea. There are storms—the water gnawing at the hull, desperately wanting to find its way inside. There are shipwrecks. But sometimes it is less dramatic but more tense. There is something moving, dark and slow, in the water beneath the boat—something you don't want to see, but you have to see it.

Otherwise, what passes for plot?

POSTCARD

That night, standing in my dining room, then our dining room, in the house where we lived, the house where I still live with our children, I slid the postcard and the notebook back into the bag, trying to put them exactly where I'd found them.

Did I go straight upstairs and confront my husband? No, I went back to the couch, opened my laptop, and googled The Addressee's name. I had to see her face. And there she was. And—*click, click, scroll*—there she was again, smiling with her children, the ones I'd read about in the notebook. They were all real, not characters in some story or play. They have names I won't use here.

It was after midnight when I shut my laptop and walked upstairs, entering our dark room. I sat down on our bed and felt him stir. What do I remember about waking him? I remember my husband being disoriented. Of course he was disoriented—his wife woke him up, using another woman's name in the dark, a name she wasn't supposed to know. Maybe you want a scene here—you want "show don't tell," you want to "see it," you want the author to "put you in the room"—but I can't build a scene from this amnesia. I can't show you because I can't see it or hear it myself. But while we're on the subject: Why would you want to be in that room with us? Why would you want to see the faded turquoise quilt on our bed, and the laundry basket full of clean, folded clothes near the closet doors, and the narrow sliver of streetlight making its way through a crack in the curtains? Maybe I'm sparing you something.

GRENADE

The night after I found the postcard and the notebook, the next night, I did it again: I checked my husband's work bag after he went up to bed. This time I didn't care who saw me—someone walking their dog after third shift, or the narrator hovering godlike above the house. I pulled out the notebook and opened to the most recent entry, but—where were the pages I'd read the night before? They were gone. I could see where they had been neatly cut out, as if with an X-Acto knife. Surgically removed. Excised.

I can only imagine what the omniscient narrator would've said about that.

That night I held the pinecone like a grenade in my hand, and then I threw it away. I threw the pinecone away, but the pinecone wasn't the problem.

A NOTE ON CONVENTIONS

After I finally read Nora Ephron's *Heartburn*, I joked to my agent on the phone, "Why didn't I think to do *that*? Why didn't I think to novelize my life?" It would've been less vulnerable, less complicated than writing this book. Yes, this could've been a novel—a tell-hers, not a tell-mine. The Wife, our protagonist, rummages through The Husband's work bag and finds a postcard addressed to a woman in another city, another state. Or maybe in the novel it's a letter, because you can do that in novels—change things. The Wife keeps looking through the bag and finds a notebook. She flips to the last written pages and reads about the woman in that other city, that other state. The Wife knows more than she's been told but less than she should.

You know what happens next: The Wife confronts her husband. She wakes him up in bed, shouting or not shouting. The reader leans in, wondering: *Will she tell him that she found the notebook?*

She doesn't. The Wife doesn't want to "catch" him, she wants to be told. The truth won't count if she has to wrestle it away from him; it will only count if he hands it to her. She wants to reach her hand out, palm open, and take it—even though she knows it will burn her hand.

The next night, The Wife returns to the notebook, the way she might press on a bruise to feel the ache of it again. But the pages she's looking for have been cut out—not torn, but neatly removed. The word that comes to mind, not a real word, is *X-Acto-ed*. The audience sees where this is going. It's going nowhere. Nowhere is the only place it can go.

There are versions of this story everywhere. When I watched *The Crown*, I held my breath a little during the scene where Elizabeth finds something in her husband's briefcase: a photograph of a woman. She says nothing. Because of her role, nothing can change.

I can't change what happened—it's not a novel, it's my life—but I'm glad at least to be living now, and here, free to make this life my own. I'm glad not to be queen.

SLEIGHT OF HAND

One afternoon I was listening to Derek DelGaudio, a master of sleight of hand, on NPR. He talked about secrets—their weight, their heft. He talked about how carrying them affects your breathing, your speech, your movements. You have to remember who knows what. You have to remember which versions of the stories you've told, and to whom, and when. If you tell the truth, there's nothing to "keep straight," nothing to work at. The truth isn't easy, but it's simple.

What I wanted from my husband was the truth. I asked for it, and I waited for it, and eventually I stopped waiting. What I was given was something different. It was shaped like it's-not-what-you-think. It held the weight of you-don't-understand.

How did I not see the heft? How did I not hear it? The question I keep asking myself is the same question we ask about someone who's good at sleight of hand: How did he *do* that?

Reader, I'm trying to give you the truth here. I'm trying to show you my hands.

SOME PEOPLE ASK

"So, how would you describe your marriage? What happened?"

Every time someone asks me a question like this, every time someone asks about my marriage, or about my divorce experience, I pause for a moment.

Inside that imperceptible pause, I'm thinking about the cost of answering fully. I'm weighing it against the cost of silence.

—I could tell the story about the pinecone, the postcard, the notebook, the face attached to the name I googled, the name I googled written in the handwriting I'd seen my name in, and the names of our children, for years and years. I could tell them how much I've spent on lawyers, or how much I've spent on therapy, or how much I've spent on dental work from grinding my teeth in my sleep, and how many hours I sleep, which is not many, but at least if I'm only sleeping a few hours a night, then I'm only grinding my teeth a few hours a night. I could talk about how a lie is worse than whatever the lie is draped over to conceal. I could talk about what a complete mindfuck it is to lose the shelter of your marriage, but also how expansive the view is without that shelter, how big the sky is—

"Sometimes people just grow apart," I say. I smile, take a sip of water. Next question.

A FRIEND SAYS EVERY BOOK BEGINS WITH AN UNANSWERABLE QUESTION

Then what is mine?
how to carry this

If we opened people up, we'd find landscapes.

—Agnès Varda

A NOTE ON SETTING

If you opened me up, you'd find Ohio. I've lived here, in a roughly heart-shaped state, all my life. The state slogan is *the heart of it all*, and I'm in the middle of the state, which means I live in the heart of the heart of it all. I'm telling you this so you know: Setting is not just *where* I am, it's who I am and what I am and why. It's not just where I live, it's *how* I live.

For me, the heart of the heart is Bexley, Ohio, a suburb just east of downtown Columbus. My house is about fifteen minutes from the hospital where I was born, where my mother was born, where my children were born. The "hospital curve" is what we call the stretch of highway 315 that wraps around Riverside Hospital, which gets its name from the Olentangy River. Fun fact: *Ohio* means "great river," so *Ohio River* means "Great River River." The "Great River River" draws the southern border of my state in thick blue ink.

I live now about twenty-five minutes from my childhood home in Westerville, a suburb just northeast of Columbus, where my parents still live. My childhood bedroom, where I wrote my first poem on loose-leaf paper, is now my father's den. A deer head hangs where my armoire once stood, knotty pine with painted green vines and red flowers winding down it. I kept my stereo behind its double doors, and all my high school CDs: The Replacements, Pixies, Liz Phair, Tori Amos, The Cure, Uncle Tupelo, The Breeders, The Sundays. On another wall, a mounted small mouth bass is frozen mid-wriggle.

My family gathers every Sunday for dinner around the same table I sat at as a child. Myself, my son and daughter, my mother, my father, my two younger sisters, their husbands, and their children—all of us gather for a meal each week, and before the divorce, my husband was there, too, sitting beside me.

HOW IT BEGAN

My husband and I became friends in an advanced creative writing workshop in college. You might want to dog-ear this detail in your mind so you can come back to it later. I never would have guessed I'd marry the person who sat directly across the seminar table from me. I was a senior; he was a junior. He was working on plays; I was writing mostly prose poems. All of us around the table wanted to be writers. I don't know if any of us thought it would actually happen, but we were there, trying.

When I graduated and moved home with my parents while applying to MFA programs, he had one year of college left. We stayed in touch: postcards, mixtapes, emails. Yes, postcards.

That fall when he came to Ohio for his senior year of college, we started meeting for Wednesday night beers at a pub about halfway between the college and my parents' house. Pints of Guinness, to be precise, and usually a basket of deep-fried pickle spears and ranch dressing. It sounds disgusting, I know, but it's delicious.

By the spring, we were a couple. Soon before he graduated, he had a short play produced in a festival at a local theater. I remember how proud I felt, seeing his picture and bio in the program with the other playwrights, and sitting beside him in the dark theater, watching actors say the words he'd written. The play was about infidelity, secrets, and betrayal. (I couldn't make this stuff up.) In the play, it slowly dawns on the poor, dumb husband what's been going on behind his back: His friend is having an affair with his wife. I don't remember how he figures it out. I don't remember how it ends.

Narrative is an accumulation of knowledge about the future.
                                                    —Sarah Ruhl

THE PLAY

Let's imagine that's what this is.

Before the play begins, before the actors take their places on the stage, something happens: the inciting incident. Offstage a man and woman walk among pines, and one of them picks up a pinecone. It's invisible to us—we don't see it—but it's what makes everything that comes next happen. It's the marble set rolling through the Rube Goldberg machine.

The play begins later, when the man's wife finds a postcard that references the pinecone. It's addressed to a woman she doesn't know in a state she's never visited. The Wife is an actor in the play but doesn't know it yet. She doesn't know the full cast. Sometimes there will seem to be no director; other times, The Husband will seem to be both starring and directing, which must be a lot of work.

It's too bad the walk through the pines has to happen before the play begins, unseen by the audience, because it would be a lovely scene for the stage—the set pieces, the music. It would have been magical, but we can only imagine it. The Wife has imagined it.

The play is about a woman who loses her husband, and in losing her husband loses her knowledge about the future. She isn't sent the script ahead of time, and no one gives her any notes. It's improv work. On the bright side, she has no lines to memorize, but she never knows what's going to happen next, or what scenes she's even supposed to be in.

In fact, no one knows what to do with a character who is called The Wife at the beginning of the play, but by the middle of the play she's no longer a wife. What should we call her character? The Snoop? The Finder? The Finder is softer, less judgmental.

The Finder didn't lose the future, only her knowledge about it. She lost the narrative. The Finder stopped knowing how to tell herself the story of her life. Where there had been a future, or at least the promise of one, there was now an ellipsis: *dot dot dot.* The ellipsis is where the sentence trails off, where you drop the thread, where the train of thought steams off in some unknown direction. The ellipsis is where you lose your partner, or your parents, or your child, or the idea of a child, or the hope for a child. The ellipsis is where you lose your house, or your job, or your health, or your appetite, or your ability to sleep. Maybe you lose twenty pounds. Maybe you lose your ability to make small talk, to act like everything is fine, to say "fine" when people ask you how you are. Maybe . . .

Dot dot dot.

And the sentence could pick up again anywhere. Or it could dissolve into silence for some time.

A NOTE ON PLOT

It's a mistake to think of my life as plot, but isn't this what I'm tasked with now—making sense of what happened by telling it as a story? Or, rather, making sense of *what is happening*. When you lose someone you love, you start to look for new ways to understand the world.

It's a mistake to visualize the narrative arc I was handed in school—inciting incident, rising action, crisis, climax, falling action, resolution, denouement—and to try to map my life onto it. It's a mistake to lay that shape over my lived experience, like a transparency the teacher would align over a worksheet, projected, so we could watch her write on it.

It is a mistake to ask oneself, *Is this falling action? Is this crisis?*

Plot is what happened, and what *happened* is one thing. What the book—the life—is *about* is another thing entirely.

THERE'S KUBRICK, AND THEN THERE'S THIS

I don't have to understand everything, and I don't believe understanding is owed me. I don't get *2001: A Space Odyssey**—fine, I can live with that. But my own life? It would be nice to get it.

---

* Seriously, what's with the apes?

LIVING IN SIN

After six months of dating, that August we moved into our first apartment in Grandview, just west of The Ohio State University campus. I wouldn't recommend moving in with anyone that quickly, but it was practical: If we wanted to stay together, we'd have to live together. I was starting graduate school in September, and he had just been hired at his first post-college job. Neither of us could afford to live alone.

That first apartment was right next to a little fast-food restaurant, Marino's Fish and Chips. When we saw Marino's spinning sign from the kitchen window, we laughed: Best Smelts in Town. We'd take it.

We moved in on a classic Ohio August day: hot and thunder-storming with torrential rain and lightning zigzagging the sky. His mother had driven in from out of state to help him move his things from his college rental house to the new apartment, but my parents, who lived just twenty minutes away, didn't offer to help. They disapproved of us moving in together for reasons that seem sensible now but hurt me then.

That first night in our new place, we cranked open the old casement window in the bedroom and stood together, watching the storm. I had one hand on the window frame when a blue flash of light bloomed around my hand, and I felt a current move through my right arm, down the side of my body and my right leg, and through my right foot. Lightning had hit the building.

I called my parents. My mother answered, and I told her what happened, no doubt full of adrenaline: "I just got hit by lightning! At the window!"

"That's what you get for living in sin," she said dryly.

So that was that. My husband and I joked for years about the black footprints burned into the beige carpet at the bedroom window. There were no footprints.

What I remember most about that apartment, apart from the spinning Marino's Fish and Chips sign, was the garish, pink-tiled bathroom. Once, when the kitchen sink was clogged and the landlord was taking his sweet time sending a plumber, we used the bathtub faucet to wash our dishes. In a photo album from those years, I have a black-and-white Polaroid of him sitting on the edge of the tub, smiling, holding a cereal bowl and a scrub brush. He's wearing a knit cap and a tee shirt that had been his in Little League—it must have been huge on him as a child, but it fit when he was twenty-two. Something about his kind eyes then remind me of my son's eyes now. He was still a boy, really. I think about how we took baths in that tub together, him sitting behind me, washing my back, and I hover like a camera on a boom over those two young people, just kids, and I pity them because they have no idea what's coming.

How I picture it: We are all nesting dolls, carrying the earlier iterations of ourselves inside. We carry the past inside us. We take ourselves—all of our selves—wherever we go.

Inside forty-something me is the woman I was in my thirties, the woman I was in my twenties, the teenager I was, the child I was.

Inside divorced me: married me, the me who loved my husband, the me who believed what we had was irrevocable and permanent, the me who believed in permanence.

I still carry these versions of myself. It's a kind of reincarnation without death: all these different lives we get to live in this one body, as ourselves.

A NOTE ON FORESHADOWING

It's a mistake to think of one's life as plot, to think of the events of one's life as events in a story. It's a mistake. And yet, there's foreshadowing everywhere, foreshadowing I would've seen myself if I'd been watching a play or reading a novel, not living a life.

THE PLAY

The Finder pictures the ellipsis as something she needs to move beyond, something she needs to cross, as if that pause—*dot dot dot*—were a canyon between mountains. She thinks she needs to send a stronger version of herself into the future, a version that can somehow leap over the chasm.

The Finder begins to write prose when she loses her husband. What does it mean to start writing prose when you've lost your narrative? Is it an attempt to build momentum, writing furiously to the right margin, building strength and speed to overcome the ellipsis, the trailing off, as if she might be able to sail over the *dot dot dot* and land on solid ground again?

What does it mean to write about trauma in real time? Instead of going to work to avoid processing the loss, The Finder makes the processing her work. She's lost her narrative, but she's writing her story. She lets the loss touch everything, as if she has a choice.

The play continues, and there's no indication of when it might end. Even if she refuses to speak, even if she refuses to move, it continues around her. Her power is limited. The curtain hasn't fallen.

HALF-DOUBLE

After graduate school I taught creative writing at Gettysburg College in Pennsylvania. It was a one-year appointment for an emerging writer. My boyfriend, not yet my husband, stayed behind in our apartment, because his job was in Columbus, and my lectureship would last only about nine months. What was the point of uprooting us both? Every few weeks, I would drive the six hours to Columbus for a long weekend, braving the specific hell that was the Pennsylvania Turnpike.

In Gettysburg I lived in an old, Civil War–era house that belonged to a professor on sabbatical for the year, and the rent was cheap because I also kept her cat alive while she was abroad. The town was full of tourists: they rode in double-decker buses or walked the streets on ghost tours, following a man in a top hat and old-timey suit, his lantern held high.

(Is that what a memoir is—a ghost tour? I'm confronting what haunts me. I'm out with lanterns, looking.)

The fall I began teaching, I was also sending out my first book manuscript, a revision of my MFA thesis. When I returned to Gettysburg after spending the winter break in Columbus, there was a message on the house's ancient woodgrain answering machine, left a week earlier: Would I please call to confirm the book was still available? I returned the editor's call, unsuspecting, and was shocked speechless when he told me my manuscript had won their annual book prize and would be published. *Lamp of the Body* would be real, in the world, in another year or so.

When I returned to Columbus full-time, we lived in a half-double on Arcadia Avenue, across from the high school my grandfather, my mother's father, had attended. This is what it is to be rooted in a place, or to have a place rooted inside you: Every bit means something to someone you know, and therefore, every bit means something to *you*.

When I moved home, instead of continuing to teach, I began working as an editor for a children's book publisher. I left that position after a couple of years for a slightly better-paying gig with a large educational publisher. Most weeks I worked ten- to twelve-hour days alongside my colleagues, all of us in our cubicles eating sad, lukewarm dinners the company had ordered in for us. I ate so much Chinese takeout at my desk, I shook out my computer keyboard over my trash can each week, watching the rice snow down. I was overworked and underpaid, but I needed the job. We weren't married, so we each had to carry our own health insurance, and besides, I was getting paid to write. Wasn't this what I wanted? Or some version of what I wanted? The version I thought I could have?

On weekends, I'd sit with my not-yet-husband at one of the coffee shops we frequented. I'd read a little, then work on poems. He'd read or work on a play. I thought of our life together as a life in words. I thought it was a beautiful life.

How I picture it: I am a half-double now—half a couple, half a whole.

A NOTE ON FORESHADOWING

My mother brought it up not long ago, how early on—maybe even when we were just friends, maybe even over pints at the pub—my husband didn't think he wanted to get married or have kids. When a friend tells you this, you don't think too much about it. Plenty of people in their early twenties can't wrap their heads around marriage and kids. But if you fall in love with that friend . . .

Dot dot dot.

And I did. I fell in love with him, and I didn't just want those things—marriage, kids, a family of my own—I wanted those things *with him.* I did what many people do when they fall in love with someone who seems to have different dreams from their own: I waited him out. I thought over time he would change his mind.

When I was in graduate school, when we were first living together in that tiny apartment where lightning struck, the apartment with the pink-tiled bathroom and Best Smelts in Town sign spinning outside the dining room window, I wrote a poem about the trepidation I was feeling. Years later, after the divorce, paging through *Lamp of the Body,* I turned to this poem and my breath caught in my throat. The word *prescient* came to mind. I knew there was a fork in the road coming, but I thought the two paths were get married, or split up. I didn't know that in time we'd do both.

AFTER READING "MOCK ORANGE"

Already, it was so:
the scent of orange blossoms
at the window, sun-jostled, bearing

the sting of the finite.
I thought of birds in those branches
as jewels, hard, refracting

light onto our walls, and knew
whatever gleaming they may have done
was not for us.

Knowledge came
disguised in sweetness
and with such ease, it astonished.

We knew, eventually, we would want
different things. Then
we started wanting them.

A FRIEND SAYS EVERY BOOK BEGINS WITH AN UNANSWERABLE QUESTION

Then what is mine?
how to set it down

BITTERSWEET

I waited him out, and it worked. It "worked." He proposed the weekend of my twenty-eighth birthday, at the little cabin in southeastern Ohio we called "our happy place." The cabin's name was Bittersweet.

At our wedding, our college creative writing professor read a poem—John Ciardi's "Most Like an Arch This Marriage." It's a poem about imperfection, about being more together than we can be on our own: "Most like an arch—two weaknesses that lean / into a strength. Two fallings become firm." Being married isn't being two columns, standing so straight and tall on their own, they never touch. Being married is leaning and being caught, and catching the one who leans toward you.

I still joke that our ceremony was really more a roast than a wedding. After reading the poem, Flanagan, as his students called him, told stories about us that had everyone laughing. "Maggie's laugh sounds like someone stepped on a crow," he said, and we all cracked up. The bride's laugh was the loudest in the room, black and feathered.

VIOLET

The year after we got married, my husband started law school. As I saw it, we took turns supporting one another, each working while the other was in graduate school. *Most like an arch.*

On a cold afternoon in December 2008, mercifully *after* law school finals, our daughter, Violet, was born. She was three days late and right on her own time. I was scheduled to be induced the night before, and I'd been told they didn't let you eat during labor (*ice chips!?*), so my plan was to fill up on some of my favorite foods before going to the hospital. I'd be prepared. We went to a diner called the Tip Top for lunch, where I had a pot roast sandwich on a pretzel roll—I wasn't yet a vegetarian—and a side of sweet potato fries. What happened next is why, to this day, I refer to the Tip Top's famous pot roast sandwich as "The Water Breaker." No, the menu hasn't been changed to reflect this.

I suspected I was leaking—just slightly—but there was no rush of water like in the movies. I felt fine. *Maybe it was nothing*, I thought. I was convinced that if we called the OB, the midwife on call would tell me to stay home until my contractions began. I'd probably still be able to have dinner at home! My heart was set on a specific burrito from the prepared section of Whole Foods (I know, right), so we headed there next.

I was standing near the salad bar, holding my coveted Brazilian shrimp burrito, when I felt it: *whoosh.* Water. I couldn't deny it this time. Did I put the burrito back and walk out? Did I rush home to pack my hospital bag? No, I stood in the checkout line in wet underwear. I'd heard about the hours and hours of ice chips and Jell-O cups in the maternity ward. *I* would be prepared. With *protein.*

I turned to my husband as we left: "Can we stop by Half Price to get a crossword book on the way home? In case I'm bored at the hospital?"

Wanting to stop at a bookstore in wet underwear was taking it too far. He drove me home, and I called the OB's office. When I described what had happened, they told me to go straight to the hospital. But my induction wasn't until 7:00 that night! It was only midafternoon! I hadn't even packed my bag yet! None of this mattered. So I threw what I thought I would need into a duffel bag—pajamas, robe, socks and underwear, toothbrush and toothpaste, face wash and contact solution, and a mix CD I'd made with *Welcome, Pickle!* written on the disc in Sharpie. (*Pickle* is what we'd been calling the baby, since seeing the first blobby ultrasound.)

At the hospital they started me on Pitocin, since I wasn't yet contracting. *Contraction* feels inadequate to describe what was happening inside me, but during labor all language was inadequate. I had never felt pain that exquisite before, and I haven't since, at least not physically. That pain, so deep inside, deep and beyond reach, made me want to jump out a plate glass window. I was in labor for twenty-four hours—stubbornly trying new positions and pushing like hell—before I accepted that the baby wasn't budging and begrudgingly agreed to a Caesarean section.

When they finally held her up, showing her to us over the surgical drape, I said, as if I recognized her from someplace, "Violet!" We'd had a short list of names for boys and for girls, but when I saw her, I knew her name. I knew her.

GROUNDS

t was the middle of winter in Ohio, bleak and washed out and bitterly cold. I would sigh a small round circle into the frosted windows, like a miniature porthole, and look out at the world I no longer felt I belonged in or to. Postpartum depression broke over me like a colossal wave almost immediately after Violet was born, though I didn't call it by its name, and I didn't treat it. It's hard to treat what you can't—or won't—name.

My husband was in his last year of law school; I was on maternity leave from my job as an editor for an educational publisher. Each day I watched the clock, waiting on edge for him to come home. How fiercely I clung to him then. How primal my love for him, how palpable my need. What had we done? We had been happy. What had I done, insisting on more of us?

We were renting a large three-bedroom Victorian house in German Village, a historic neighborhood of Columbus known for its brick streets, horse hitching posts, gas lamps, and manicured gardens. Our house was built in the late 1800s. Each day I did our laundry in a cramped cellar with low ceilings and a dirt floor. There were so many burp cloths and bibs crusty and sour with spit-up, so many unmatched socks the size of my thumb, so many pairs of footed pajamas, so many receiving blankets. Bags of labeled breastmilk in the freezer. Naps scheduled and hoped for, desperately hoped for, and missed. Outgoing mail I had no stamps for.

Outside the trees were encased in ice, the branches clacking against each other. What spark was I supposed to feel each day in waking up, tipping the whistling kettle over the coffee grounds, warm and wet and black as soil, then trudging, hunched over, to the basement to do more laundry? What spark was I supposed to feel in making a bottle, then another bottle, then another bottle? How sad the kettle sounded when I removed it from the flame—how it whined before it grew quiet, went silent.

I didn't write for the first year of Violet's life. Strike that: I *couldn't* write. I was sleep deprived and anxious and, I know now, suffering from something with a name. Something I could have treated. The land of poems felt impossibly far away; I could barely make it out on the horizon and had no idea how to get there. Even if I'd known the way, even if I'd had a map, when could I have made that journey?

After a year, the first poem finally arrived.

FIRST FALL

I'm your guide here. In the evening-dark
morning streets, I point and name.
Look, the sycamores, their mottled,
paint-by-number bark. Look, the leaves
rusting and crisping at the edges.
I walk through Schiller Park with you
on my chest. Stars smolder well
into daylight. Look, the pond, the ducks,
the dogs paddling after their prized sticks.
Fall is when the only things you know
because I've named them
begin to end. Soon I'll have another
season to offer you: frost soft
on the window and a porthole
sighed there, ice sleeving the bare
gray branches. The first time you see
something die, you won't know it might
come back. I'm desperate for you
to love the world because I brought you here.

THE PLAY

There's only so much the audience gets to see.

When we meet The Wife and The Husband, the worst has happened, at least from The Wife's perspective. We come to them in crisis. But what about before?

We don't get to see the before. There isn't enough time, enough stage, enough set pieces for the before. The audience doesn't get to see The Husband and The Wife pack up and leave the old house in German Village. There is no monologue about how they don't want to give up city living, but they need a good school district for The Daughter. They don't want to sell their *whole* souls, The Wife jokes to her friends.

The audience doesn't get to see The Husband and The Wife going to open houses with their real estate agent. We don't see the look on The Wife's face when she drives down the street with the periwinkle house for sale. It's like driving down a tunnel of trees, she thinks, but there is no voice-over to give us her thoughts. We only get her words and actions. Only the things we can see and hear.

There's no program for the play—it's only an imagined play, after all—and therefore no asterisked note in the program about Bexley, Ohio, being the only city in the country designated as an arboretum. So many trees, some of them pines. So many pinecones.

The Husband and The Wife buy a house and move in just after The Daughter's first birthday. The periwinkle house—"like the crayon from the 64-color box," The Wife likes to say, "the one with the built-in sharpener"—is in walking distance of the elementary school The Daughter eventually attends. It's walkable to coffee shops, restaurants, the pharmacy, the public library, the post office, the art house movie theatre. The Husband and The Wife sell only a *percentage* of their souls.

When they move into the house, it's winter, a new year. The Husband is an associate attorney at a law firm. The Wife is still an editor, working a regular forty-hour week. The Daughter is in daycare full-time. Each day The Wife drops her off in the morning on her way to the office and picks her up on her way home.

This is where The Wife becomes more mother than wife. There is a shift. If there were a program for this imagined play, we would change her name again on the cast page.

A NOTE ON CHARACTER

The Wife—The Mother, The Finder—would love to be someone who doesn't give a fuck, or who at least gives considerably fewer fucks, but she is not that person. That's not how she was built. The Wife's factory setting is GAF. She gives so many fucks. All the fucks.

A NOTE ON BETRAYAL

Here's the thing: Betrayal is neat. It absolves you from having to think about your own failures, the ways you didn't show up for your partner, the harm you might have done.

Betrayal is neat because no matter what else happened—if you argued about work or the kids, if you lacked intimacy, if you were disconnected and lonely—it's as if that person doused everything with lighter fluid and threw a match.

Sometimes I wonder: If there had been no postcard, no notebook, would our marriage have survived?

I don't know. That's the truth.

THE LEAP

When Violet was two, I quit my job in educational publishing. I didn't know if I could hack it as a freelancer, but I wanted a different life for myself, as a mother and as a writer. I was finally ready to try.

For seven years, I'd been working full-time as an editor. I'd published one book of poems and was plugging away at a second manuscript. My writing time was compressed: I wrote on my lunch hour in my cubicle and in the evenings on my couch after my toddler was asleep. Those afternoons spent writing and reading at coffee shops with my husband? Long gone. Family time was compressed, too: my husband and I were with Violet for dinner and bath and bedtime, then again first thing in the morning, in that mad, getting-ready rush, but the bulk of our days we spent apart, the three of us in three different places.

I watched from my desk as the freelance writers and editors who worked for the company walked in and out of the building. They were doing what I was doing, but they were doing it from home. I'd think, *When they meet a deadline, they can stop for the day. They can work on a project of their own. They can take their kids to the zoo.* When I finished my own tasks, I couldn't just clock out. My reward for being efficient was more work—often the tasks of coworkers—to keep me busy until it was time for me to leave.

When Violet was two years old, I received thrilling news: I'd been awarded a Creative Writing Fellowship from the National Endowment for the Arts. I remember getting the call, jumping up and down in the kitchen with my husband, and scooping toddler Violet up into my arms. We danced and celebrated together, the three of us.

The federal government had invested in me as a poet, and I wanted to honor that. I wanted to invest in myself, too. I wanted to attend a writing residency—to immerse myself in a project for a couple of weeks—but it wasn't possible with the amount of vacation time I had accrued. I'd had to use vacation time to care for my daughter whenever she was sick, and two-year-olds in daycare are often sick, so those days dwindled quickly.

I asked my boss if I could transition to freelancing for the company. The answer was no.

I asked if I could transition to part-time, without benefits, since we were on my husband's benefits anyway. The answer was no.

I asked if I could stay on as a full-time employee, but take some unpaid leave for a writing residency. The answer was no.

I had a difficult decision to make. I weighed the risk against the potential rewards, and I decided to take a leap. I bet on myself. I quit.

I knew I wouldn't be freelancing for the company I was leaving, but I could find other clients—and I did. The NEA grant in the bank was my safety net. If my work dried up, we'd have that money until I figured out a Plan B. Over the next several years, I spent the grant on writing-related expenses—manuscript submission fees, conference registrations, travel for readings—but I didn't need a Plan B (or C, or D, or E).

Soon after leaving my job, I attended my first residency at the Virginia Center for the Creative Arts, where I completed my second book, *The Well Speaks of Its Own Poison*, and began work on some of the poems that would be included in my third book, *Good Bones*. That experience was transformative for me. I was *in it*—immersed, dedicated. I was *really doing it*. At VCCA I met writers, composers, and visual artists from all over the country who were really doing it, too.

I befriended Kathy, a paper artist from Baltimore, and I was inspired to write the hawk-and-girl poems in *Good Bones* after seeing her intricate work. I met Dennis, a composer living in New York City, and we've since collaborated on not one but two pieces pairing my words with his music. To this day, I'm grateful for the sense of community I had with other artists there—Kathy, Dennis, Marie, Sally, Dan, Olive, Jim, Peggy, and Walter, among others; the cross-pollination that happened during the residency; and the creative momentum that carried me long after I left.

I was supposed to be at VCCA for two full weeks. But on the ninth night, I woke up around 2:00 in the morning and felt inexplicably frantic. I had no idea why, but I knew I had to leave. I packed my things, left a bottle of wine and a note for my new friends, and slipped outside.

It was pouring rain on Mt. San Angelo, and the road winding down the mountain had no guardrails, and there were deer crossings, and I had to creep along to stay on the road, but I kept going. I drove straight through to Bexley, about seven hours, and arrived at my house late morning. I knew it was naptime at the daycare, so I waited an hour, then went to pick up Violet. I cried when I saw her. We both cried. She looked somehow different, older, to me.

Later, talking to my husband about how Violet did while I was gone, he told me she'd been fine all week but had woken up around 2:00 that morning, crying, inconsolable.

This is a story about magical thinking. She called me down off the mountain in the rain.

THE MATERIAL

At a women's clinic about a mile from my house, blocks from my children's elementary school, anti-choice activists regularly stand outside with large signs. The signs say 8 Weeks, 10 Weeks, 12 Weeks, each with a picture of a tiny, bloody person. I've miscarried in that time frame, not once but twice, and not once but twice there was no tiny, bloody person.

The first time I miscarried, we rushed to the ER, hoping the blood didn't mean what we thought it did. My parents came to the house to watch Violet while we were at the hospital, and I remember coming home in the wee hours of the morning, finding them both asleep on our couch, and hugging them, sobbing. In the weeks afterward, there were tests, tests, and more tests. We were told what most people are probably told: "This happens. Keep trying."

Then it happened again. I was in the bathroom at work when I started bleeding, and I quickly gathered my things from my cubicle and drove home in tears. This time, there was what they call "material."

I called my husband: "Oh my god, there's something in the blood, something firm."

I called my OB's office: "It's happening again, but it's worse this time."

The triage nurse asked what I'm sure were routine questions, but they felt anything but routine: "Are you passing anything other than blood? Any fetal material?"

"Yes," I told her. "Do I need to keep it? Could it be tested to see what's wrong?"

"Collect what you can," she said.

"How much should I try to keep?" The absurdity of the question. The cruelty.

I don't remember what she said.

I put the "material" in a small Tupperware container. I had no idea where I should keep it. In the fridge? And where in the fridge do you keep your Tupperware container of "material"?

I have no idea what I did with it. I don't remember if I took it to the doctor, threw it out, or flushed it down the toilet. I can remember the dress I wore to my eighth birthday party—beige with tiny blue flowers, a bib collar with a thin blue ribbon tied into a bow, long sleeves with ruffles at the wrists—but I don't remember what I did with the fetal material from my second miscarriage. The mind is mysterious. A master of sleight of hand.

What I do remember is the well-meaning woman in the waiting room at the OB's office afterward. She was sitting there, clearly pregnant, with two young boys. I was sitting next to my husband on the other side of the room. She smiled and said, "Are you having a baby?"

"No," I said. She looked away.

I also remember the other people who said, later, trying to comfort me, "At least you never knew the baby." Meaning: At least you didn't meet the baby, hold the baby, name the baby, love the baby. At least the baby wasn't part of your family.

There is a difference between what is built in the body and what is built in the imagination. I'd already considered myself a mother of two. I'd already thought of Violet as a big sister. I'd put in notice at my job, intending to start my freelance career so I could devote more time to my writing that year and stay home with my new baby the next. But no, I wasn't having a baby. And no, I never knew the baby. And no, I didn't hold the baby, unless the Tupperware container counts. It doesn't count.

HERE WE GO AGAIN

It was Valentine's Day, a few months after the second miscarriage, and I was watching the pink word *pregnant* form in the tiny window on the test. I placed the plastic test in a long box, the kind you might open to find a nice pen or a bracelet, and wrapped it. I asked my husband to come home for lunch, because I couldn't wait to give him his present.

We were standing together in the dining room when he opened the box and saw the positive pregnancy test inside. His reaction: "Here we go again." I can't say hope was the dominant emotion—I'm trying to tell you the truth here. Neither of us knew what would happen, but I think we both felt like the odds were against us. This would be our last chance for another child. We wouldn't put ourselves—and I wouldn't put my body—through this again.

Every day, I scanned the horizon for storms, hypervigilant. I didn't believe my eyes when they saw nothing.

To strip away the metaphor: Every day for nine months, I expected blood. From the very beginning, I expected the end. That sort of thing changes you.

How I picture it: Inside current me, the me who has two children, is the me who dreamed two others. The me who lived in fear, then grief, then fear, then grief again, then fear.

RHETT

When Violet was born, I had expectations. I had a detailed birth plan with bullet points, which I laugh about now, because after twenty-four hours of labor the birth plan became "get the baby out alive" (sort of like, after bringing home a newborn who had colic, acid reflux, and a dairy sensitivity, the parenting plan became "by any means necessary").

With Rhett, I knew what to expect. Because Violet had been a large baby and I had experienced some complications, the midwife explained that I wasn't a good candidate for a VBAC—a vaginal birth after Caesarian. This time the surgery was scheduled. The night before our son arrived, my husband and I went to Lindey's, a swishy bistro in the brick-paved German Village neighborhood where we'd lived when Violet was born, and I had my favorite—tournedos of beef, mashed potatoes, asparagus. Rather, I ate half and took the other half home. I would be prepared.

My OB told me I could eat ten hours before my surgery, which was at noon. I did the math and set an alarm for 1:45 A.M. When it went off, I tiptoed downstairs, heated up my meal in the microwave, and scarfed down half a steak dinner alone in the dark at the dining room table. My husband's mother was visiting, and she was asleep on the daybed in the front room. I ate quickly and quietly, brushed my teeth, and went back to bed.

When I arrived at the hospital, the anesthesiologist came in with a clipboard and asked me all the standard questions while checking off boxes and making notes.

"When did you last eat?" he asked, barely looking up.

"Around two this morning," I said.

"Okay, what did you have?"

I think this is the part where he expected me to say a bowl of cereal or some cheese and crackers or even a little ice cream.

"Steak and potatoes," I told him. "And a little asparagus."

He stopped writing and looked up from his paperwork. I remember the look on his face—incredulous, borderline angry.

"Push Pepcid in her IV," he told the nurse, clearly annoyed. "I hate when doctors tell their patients they can do this shit. I'll never be able to use your name, because it would be a HIPAA violation, but you'd better believe I'll be telling this story—the one about the woman who set an alarm to eat steak at two in the morning."

In the delivery room, he told me he was the anesthesiologist for the gorillas at the Columbus Zoo. All gorillas had C-sections, apparently. If he could handle the gorillas, he could handle the 2:00 A.M. steak woman.

But lying there, feeling them tugging at me on the other side of the surgical drape, I started to listen to my heart rate, and I could hear it beating erratically. I'd experienced some arrhythmia off and on since I was pregnant with Violet. I'd written about it after she was born, in a poem spoken directly to her. "Shapeshifter" opens, "Half me, you're half haunted. Your heart is destined to skip / like a scratched record."

I had an echocardiogram when I was pregnant with Violet, and the doctors hadn't seemed overly concerned with the results. My blood volume was enormous thanks to the baby, they said, so the issue would probably resolve after pregnancy. There in the room, though, my pulse beeping loudly on the machine didn't sound *resolved*. It sounded more like hiccups than a regular, steady heartbeat.

"Something's wrong—something's wrong with my heart," I said. I started to panic. I wasn't breathing deeply enough, and my hands started going numb. I was hyperventilating. In that moment, my mind rushed to the darkest place. I thought I was going to die.

The anesthesiologist crouched down beside me, on my left side—my husband was on my right—and talked me through it. It was okay, he kept telling me. Breathe. I was going to be fine. I was given some oxygen through a mask. My heart found its regular rhythm.

Just a few minutes later, when they pulled Rhett from my body, I heard a nurse say, "The head just keeps on coming!"

Someone else said, "Who guessed the higher weight, Mom or Dad?"

I had, so I won the bet. Our boy was 9 pounds, 8 ounces, and over 21 inches long. He went straight into size 1 Pampers in the delivery room, bypassing newborn diapers altogether. He had thick, dark hair and sideburns—like a little Elvis impersonator. His cry was low and gruff.

The next morning, when my parents brought Violet to the hospital room to meet her brother for the first time, she crawled up into my hospital bed. I was holding the baby, and I turned him to show her. "Violet, this is Rhett."

"Like Rhett Miller?" she asked, mooning at him. We listened to Rhett Miller and his band, Old 97's, all the time.

"Yep, like Rhett Miller. That's exactly right." I laughed. "Violet, you're so rock and roll."

HERE COMES THE SUN

We all come into the world less than done, unfinished, our skulls still stitching themselves together. We have soft spots. *Fontanelle* means "little fountain," because of the pulsing you can see.

Rhett was the child who almost wasn't, the last child we would ever have. If we'd believed in miracles, he would've been one. He was the sun, the light at the end of a long darkness. At first he was so calm and quiet, I thought the curse was broken. He slept and slept, only waking to nurse. But after a couple of weeks, he emerged from the fog of birth. He screamed. He refused to close his eyes, let alone sleep. Hour after hour, I carried him around, swaying his swaddled body as he blinked up at me, utterly awake and alert. He slept maybe six hours out of any twenty-four-hour period, but in brutal twenty-minute increments. I found myself at the edge again, but this time with a four-year-old to care for.

Why wouldn't the baby sleep? What was upsetting his stomach? What could I do for him that would help? Desperate for answers, I wrote everything down: every feeding, what time he started, what time he finished, when he burped, when he spit up, what the spit-up looked like, when he peed, when he pooped, what the poop looked like, when he cried, what his cry sounded like, when he slept, what position he slept in, when he woke.

If I wrote everything down, I would see The Pattern. The Pattern That Would Make Him Happy. The Pattern That Would Make Him Sleep. The Pattern That Would Fix Him. The Pattern That Would Fix Me.

The books all say to sleep when the baby sleeps. But what if the baby doesn't sleep? What then, books? When my son napped, in tiny spurts, I spent those few minutes scribbling down everything that had happened since my last entry. Then he'd wake, screaming, and I'd set down the notebook.

I sang my son "Close Your Eyes" and "Fire and Rain" by James Taylor, because I knew the words, because they were sad and beautiful and so were we. I sang him "Here Comes the Sun," as if singing it could make it so. We all come into the world less than done, unfinished, little fountains.

This time I had no office to escape to. I'd left my job in publishing to begin a freelance career the previous year, so I'd have more time and flexibility as a parent. I decided that if I couldn't change my life, I would order it. I created a schedule and became a slave to it: set feedings, set ounces, set "naptimes" (swaddled, carried around, propped precariously in a bouncer or swing, only to wake seconds later). I couldn't leave the house. I had to stay home, keep him on track, offer him naps in his own crib. I had to swaddle, shush, sway.

I had to find The Pattern. The Pattern That Would Fix Us.

That winter was bitter cold. I was a recluse with a reflux baby who fussed and cried and rarely slept. My friends left fresh-ground coffee from the local coffee shop on the stoop, or they stayed and kept me company as I paced the carpet, bouncing and shushing my swaddled, blinking baby in my arms.

When my husband told me to call my doctor, when he told me that my frantic listing wasn't normal, that my anger wasn't normal, I vented to my friends. There is no parenting-a-newborn medication, I insisted. My life is hard, and there is no pill to make a hard life easy. I remember saying that, almost verbatim.

Then one January morning, angry that my husband invited friends over for brunch, friends I couldn't face, I started cleaning. I picked up toys from the living room carpet and threw them into the playroom. The air sizzled. My husband texted our friends to cancel. As he whisked Violet away for an errand, I heard her say, on the way out the door, "Let's go, I don't want to be around Mom. She's mad all the time."

I was. I was furious. Where was my bundle of joy—again? How could this happen twice? After all I'd been through to have this child, why couldn't I just be grateful?

I drove around for maybe an hour that night, between feedings, because the car was the only place where I could be alone and sob, where I couldn't hear a baby, where I could turn the music up loud.

They call it *extinction*: letting a baby cry it out, letting a baby cry until he can't cry anymore, until he gives up and finally sleeps. I let myself cry it out. I was extinct?

The next day I made the appointment with my OB-GYN's office. I didn't want to be that mother. I already felt guilty, as if I had cheated on my daughter by having another child. I couldn't betray her again by changing, by having her lose the mother she'd had for four years, the kind, patient mother she loved and counted on.

The nurse asked if I had thought of harming the baby or myself. Was I eating, was I sleeping, was I exercising, was I going out with friends? No, I told her. No, no, no, no. I wasn't sad; I was mad. I couldn't turn myself off. I couldn't fix my son.

She looked at my chart. I'd been pregnant three times in two years. It makes sense, but I hadn't known it until then: Miscarriage is a predictor for postpartum anxiety and depression. Of course you feel out of control: Your hormones have been all over the place. You've been heartbroken, wrung out, exhausted, and scared. You can't make your body do what it should, and now you can't make your child do what he should.

The nurse prescribed a low dose of Lexapro and asked to see me back in sixty days. It would take a few weeks for me to feel results, and it would be thirty days before the medication reached therapeutic level in my system.

The treatment itself was something to endure: the flat feeling, like monotone. I'd always felt high highs, low lows. I'd always been black or white. But Lexapro was gray, gray, gray. I listened to sad songs, alarmed that they didn't make me feel sad. They didn't make me feel anything. The flat gray, the deadening, was worth it—for my kids, for my marriage, for me—and eventually it gave way to shades of gray. There were almost whites, almost blacks.

Now I can't find the notebook I kept when Rhett was a newborn. His father threw it away, or I threw it away, or it threw itself away. I know what I would not find there: answers. There are no answers. We're all little fountains—soft, pulsing. We all come into the world unfinished, still stitching ourselves together.

A NOTE ON INCITING INCIDENTS

Once upon a time, people believed in something called "maternal impression." If anything was wrong with a child, that error could be traced back to the mother.

When Joseph Merrick was born, some people believed his mother caused his deformities. When she was pregnant with him, she was scared by an elephant.

I sang my son "Close Your Eyes" and "Fire and Rain" by James Taylor, then worried that the melodies would depress him, that the notes would somehow change his wiring. Or was he already wired to be like me: too raw for the world, nerves too close to the skin?

How I picture it: The past is stacked ceiling-high, and we have to pack and label everything using only our teeth. We have to pack it all if we want to carry it forward.

Imagine all there is for us to sort: years and years and years. Moldering cardboard and mice nesting in it. One child, then two.

A NOTE ON THE AUTHOR'S INTENTION

When Violet was in preschool, building things with cardboard and string and glitter glue, she called her creations *revengines*.

I think it was simply a mishearing—a bad translation from what she'd heard and meant to say, *inventions*—but the word sparked my imagination. What was my four-year-old assembling at our dining room table, sitting up on her knees on a chair? An engine powered by revenge?

As a writer, I've never made a *revengine*, nor would I want to. This book you're holding is not powered by anger, but by curiosity and a desire to understand. ("I am out with lanterns, looking for myself.") This book is powered by questions, many of them unanswerable, so their fuel burns forever.

A FRIEND SAYS EVERY
BOOK BEGINS WITH AN
UNANSWERABLE QUESTION

Then what is mine?
how to forgive

AN OFFERING

feel like I need to reiterate something: This isn't the story of a good wife and a bad husband. Was I easy to live with? Probably not. I craved time to myself. I thought I knew best what the children needed. I was stubborn. I disliked—*dislike*—confrontation, so I could be—*can be*—avoidant or passive-aggressive. If you hurt my feelings, I might have carried that pain quietly, but the quiet was loud. I had postpartum depression twice, and I miscarried twice, and I suffered, and that suffering was loud.

My husband and I said to one another, on different and various occasions: "I'm not your staff." We were both right, and both angry, and maybe both wrong to be angry. It doesn't matter now.

This is also true: I was—*am*—loving, honest, dependable, funny, compassionate, and loyal. But I was not my best self in my marriage, at least not toward the end.

After the divorce I came across the writings of the Buddhist teacher Chögyam Trungpa. As a man, he was problematic. He drank too much, slept around, and didn't live as we'd expect a great, wise teacher to live. But every teacher is human. Likewise, parents are not wise oracles—they're just people trying to shepherd other people through the world. We may know the right path to take, but knowing the way and consistently walking it are two different things. Everything we learn, we learn from someone who is imperfect.

Trungpa writes about *torma* and *don*. "Possession" is the closest translation for the Tibetan word *don*—a ghost that causes misfortune, anger, fear, sickness. When you have a don, *you* are the possession. The anger possesses—*owns*—you.

Torma means "offering cake." You offer the torma to your don. You feed the ghost that does you harm, "that which possesses you." Giving it a little something sweet is a way of saying, *Thank you for the pain you caused me, because that pain woke me up. It hurt enough to make me change.* "Wish for more pain," a friend's therapist once told her, "because that's how you'll change." It has to hurt so much that you have to do something differently. The pain forces your hand.

When I read Trungpa, I thought about my own ghosts differently. Fear isn't inside me, *I'm* inside *it*. Anger isn't something I'm holding; it's something that's held *me*, possessed *me*. And being possessed is the opposite of being free.

By the time you're reading this sentence, I want to have let go, to have wrestled myself free of this ghost, to have forgiven. I want to be able to say, Thank you, pain, for being my teacher.

This book is my torma, my offering. Please take it. Taste its sweetness.

A NOTE ON FORESHADOWING

It's a mistake to think of one's life as plot, but there's foreshadowing everywhere. When my husband introduced me at the release party for my second book of poems, I was standing off to the side of the stage, my arm around our daughter, holding her close. As he said many kind things about me, I remember thinking, *Huh*. What he said about me and my writing in public felt different than his attitude at home.

This story could have begun so many places. It could have begun there, in that room, with all of those people watching. *He's so proud of her*, some of them probably thought. *They're so happy together.*

It's easy to see the beginnings of things, and harder to see the ends.

—Joan Didion

HIDDEN PICTURES

In the fall of 2015 I sat in a chair in a coffee shop and wrote a poem on a legal pad, which is where most of my poems begin. I titled it "Good Bones." The poem was published online in the journal *Waxwing* the following June—the same week as the Pulse Nightclub massacre in Orlando and the murder of MP Jo Cox in England.

You're reading this book, so you probably know what happened next: the poem went viral. Reporters emailed, messaged me on social media, called. Meanwhile, I was parenting two children, ages three and seven. I was *Violet's mom* and *Rhett's mom* most of all—that was how I was known to people in my life, and that was fine with me. Even after the poem went viral, I was still hidden, cleverly disguised as one of the least visible creatures on earth: a middle-aged mother. As I told a reporter from the *Columbus Dispatch*, my hometown paper, "I feel like I go into a phone booth and I turn into a poet sometimes. Most of the other time, I'm just Maggie who pushes the stroller."

It's cynical to think the end of a thing is tucked inside its beginning, like the hidden pictures in a *Highlights* magazine—an umbrella, a pencil, a roller skate. Or a pinecone, a postcard, a poem. But my marriage was never the same after that poem.

GOOD BONES

Life is short, though I keep this from my children.
Life is short, and I've shortened mine
in a thousand delicious, ill-advised ways,
a thousand deliciously ill-advised ways
I'll keep from my children. The world is at least
fifty percent terrible, and that's a conservative
estimate, though I keep this from my children.
For every bird there is a stone thrown at a bird.
For every loved child, a child broken, bagged,
sunk in a lake. Life is short and the world
is at least half terrible, and for every kind
stranger, there is one who would break you,
though I keep this from my children. I am trying
to sell them the world. Any decent realtor,
walking you through a real shithole, chirps on
about good bones: This place could be beautiful,
right? You could make this place beautiful.

THIS WASN'T THE DEAL

One night, lying next to me in bed, my husband told me I was famous. He said it quietly in the dark. In his inflection, I heard sadness. I heard *you're not the same anymore, you're gone somehow.*

"I'm not famous," I said. "I just wrote a famous poem." It wasn't the same thing.

I said it as a kind of apology, as reassurance, because I felt like I'd been accused of something. In my inflection, I hoped he'd hear *I'm the same, I'm just me, I'm right here.*

ON SECOND THOUGHT

'm trying to tell you the truth here, so let me go back: I said it was enough to be a mother. No, I said it was enough to be *known* as a mother. To be mostly invisible. But was it enough for me to know I was a poet? Is it ever enough if our inner lives, and our lives aside from being parents, are just that—inner lives, lives aside? Hidden pictures?

I wonder: How will my children feel if they think that being seen as a mother wasn't enough for me? What will they think of me, knowing I wanted a full life—a life with them and a life in words, too?

I'm dog-earing a realization in my mind now: I don't think fathers are asking themselves these questions. Fathers don't feel guilty for wanting an identity apart from their children, because the expectation is that they have lives outside of the home. I'm starring and underlining this fact for future reference.

SOME PEOPLE WILL ASK

"Why are you telling these stories? Why air your dirty laundry?" Someone will ask this, or if they don't ask, they'll think it. Maybe you're thinking it now. How do I answer?

—I could say what happened to me is mine. I could say that suffering equals pain plus resistance, and I'm no longer resisting, no longer holding it in, letting it fester. And why would you expect me, or anyone, to grit my teeth and quietly carry my story? I could say there is a cost to carrying your truth but not telling it. I could say women have been doing this for decades and look where it's landed us. I could say I've gone and lost my narrative, and lost not only my understanding of the future but also my understanding of the past, and this is how I'm trying to find it—

"Who's calling this laundry dirty, anyway? It's just lived-in." Next question.

THE BULLY WON?

Every year since becoming a mother—or at least every year until the pandemic—I took my children with me to vote. I have pictures of me standing at a voting machine in their elementary school gym, a stroller parked beside me. I have pictures of us on the walk home, I Voted stickers on our jackets. Violet and Rhett have always been happy to come along, in large part because of the bake sale that PTO sets up in the elementary school gym—cupcakes, cookies, and brownies for a dollar each. And poll workers always willing to give out extra stickers.

But Election Day 2016 was different. It felt different—more charged, more important. Violet, then in second grade, was thrilled to come along with me. It was just the two of us that time, because we were going to vote for the first female president. I wore my Not Today, Patriarchy tee shirt; hers read Future President. I made my selections at the machine, but I let Violet push the large button to cast my—our—ballot for change.

I was teary that day, feeling the historical significance of the moment, but also remembering holding her as a newborn as I watched Barack Obama's inauguration. I voted for Barack Obama while incredibly pregnant with Violet, and she had been in the world for about three weeks when he was sworn in. In January 2009 I felt hope. In November 2016 I felt it, too.

That night I tucked in Violet at her regular bedtime, but I promised I'd wake her up when Hillary Clinton won, so we could celebrate the first Madam President together. Needless to say, I didn't wake her up. She slept in her bedroom upstairs, unaware of how her country was changing, and I stayed up until almost 3:30 in the morning, willing a different outcome— talk about magical thinking. I sobbed on the couch, then fell asleep there. The next morning I woke to find Violet standing in front of me.

She knew. "The bully won?" she asked, incredulous, almost accusingly. As in: *How could this happen?* In the books she'd read and the movies she'd watched at that point, the hero or heroine always prevailed. Nothing in her experience had prepared her for the possibility that the right, good thing might not happen.

My daughter was shocked because she believed—and I had led her to believe—that people are good. And that there is consensus about what "good" is. That the choice is always clear. But most of the time, "good" and "bad" aren't so easy to discern. In stories there are good guys and bad guys. In life there are people in pain, people who are broken and making decisions from a place of brokenness, people living with wounds we can't see—and these people, these fallible human beings, are our mothers and fathers, our husbands and wives, our sisters and brothers, our children, our teachers.

Election night, when the results were clear, I turned off the news and sobbed into my dog's impossibly soft neck, because she let me, and soon I was crying and cursing the son of a bitch who starved and beat her.

When we first brought Phoebe home, we could see her hips, spine, rib cage—hooks and ladders of bone. Her legs were shaved from surgery, bite-scarred. The rescue agency said another dog in the home chewed her leg to the bone, and the owners left the wound to abscess. She was a terrified creature, but she's a different animal now. We're both different animals now.

NOT THAT ONE

I don't keep a diary or journal, so if I want to remember the contours and textures of my daily life from a certain time, the easiest way back is to look at my social media. My Instagram feed from April 2017 shows a picture of my TV screen, with the "Good Bones" episode of *Madam Secretary* cued up on the DVR, sandwiched between photos of four-year-old Rhett tracing print letters in a practice workbook.

It comes rushing back—how he insisted on playing school each day, envious of how his sister went off to "real" school while he attended part-time preschool at our local JCC. I set up the dining room table like a desk— workbook, pencils, erasers—and would sit there waiting for him to arrive on the school bus. Sure enough, I'd hear plastic wheels on the hardwood floors and would look up to see Rhett on his little scooter—a makeshift bus. I'd welcome my son to "school," and he'd climb up into a chair and do a page or two, meticulously tracing the letters and numbers. I'd bring him a snack, maybe a box of raisins, as he worked. As the teacher in this role play, I'd praise his careful penmanship and then "grade" the pages, drawing a big star in red marker at the top of the page or adding a sticker if I had one handy.

That night, April 9, after the rush of dinner and bath time and stories and tuck-ins, my husband and I sat down and watched *Madam Secretary* on CBS. We'd bought a bottle of champagne, which we'd nearly finished, full of nervous energy, before the episode aired. All I'd been told by the writer, Joy Gregory, was that my poem would appear at the end of the episode, which was also called "Good Bones." I didn't know until watching it live that night which character would read the poem, or how it would be incorporated into the scene. Because the poem had gone viral online, I assumed it would be shared on a character's computer screen or phone. Because the speaker of the poem is a mother, I subconsciously expected a woman to share the poem.

I was caught off guard when Sebastian Arcelus, who played Chief of

Staff Jay Whitman, took his wallet from his pocket and removed a small piece of paper. My poem. It wasn't something a staff member emailed to another, not something one of the characters pulled up on social media. No, it was something this character took the time to print and carry with him always, a kind of talisman, and that leveled me. I covered my face and cried, missing the scene entirely, and then had to rewind and rewatch it.

Other photos from that week and the week to follow: art from the JCC hallway, the kids and me at the park, a trip to Virginia for a reading in Charlottesville, a mother-daughter lunch date with Violet. The cover reveal of my third book, *Good Bones*, was dated April 17. Two days later, April 19, I came into the house after a rare treat for me, an evening pedicure, wearing flip-flops, those pink foam contraptions stuffed awkwardly between my toes. Standing in my living room, I looked down at my phone and gasped.

Saeed Jones had tweeted at me. *Yo, @maggiesmithpoet: Meryl Streep read your poem "Good Bones" tonight at the @POETSorg gala and we're all dead now. Thank you!*

I had to read it again. *Meryl Streep?! Where? What?*

I immediately googled *Meryl Streep Lincoln Center*, and there it was: the event that night was the Academy of American Poets' annual gala. Meryl Streep, one of the presenters, had read my poem to close the event. Wait, *what?* While I was standing in my living room in Ohio wearing flip-flops and pink foam toe-spreaders, my name and my poem were in Meryl Streep's mouth?

If someone had told me, when I wrote "Good Bones" on a legal pad in a coffee shop, on just some weeknight I'd managed to get out of the house after the kids went to bed, that *Meryl Fucking Streep* would be reading it at Lincoln Center, I wouldn't have believed it. Who would have believed it?

While video recording hadn't been authorized, I was able to listen to the audio. I sat at my dining room table and listened to an unmistakable voice say, "A poem by Maggie Smith." And when there was an audible murmuring in the audience, the voice said, "Not that one. The *American*."

"Not that one" is a title I claim proudly. I'm the other one.

In the following days, I can see from my social media posts that life continued as normal: I baked with the kids, took them out to coffee shops for their favorite treats, captured sidewalk chalk drawings in my neighborhood while walking the dog, went to visit my parents, saw Guided By Voices play at a small club on a weeknight.

Meryl Streep can read your poem, and it can be in an episode of a primetime TV show, but your life is still your life—mothering and dog-walking and working. The things we call "life-changing" are and aren't.

A NOTE ON FORESHADOWING

I've been thinking about how sometimes we write the truth before we know it. Once, during the Q&A after a reading from *Good Bones*, someone in the audience raised her hand and asked me about writing the experience of a single mother. What was it like, she wanted to know, being a single mother and writing about that in my poetry?

"I'm not a single mother!" I said, and laughed. I wasn't, not yet, but I would be later that year. I had no idea that was coming. I was—nearly happily? somewhat precariously?—married, but I hadn't written about my husband in the book. His absence hadn't occurred to me until that moment. As I see it now, *Good Bones* is a love letter to my children and my mother.

Remember when I said this story could have begun so many places? It could have begun there, at the reading, or it could have begun more than a year later, in Tucson, Arizona, when I was poet-in-residence at the University of Arizona Poetry Center. By then I was a newly single mother. My ex-husband wasn't officially my ex-husband yet, but he had moved out a few weeks earlier. One night while I was in Tucson, I got a message from my poet-friend Sonia. She wrote something that has stuck with me: how *prescient* the book *Good Bones* was, because I had written the experience of being a single mother before I lived it. Or maybe I had lived some version of single motherhood both on and off the page before it was official.

At the reading earlier that year, when the woman asked about me being a single mother, I'd laughed it off as an entertaining story: *How funny, she thought I was single!* But what is this story now? How do I feel about that question now, knowing what I know, living the way I do, alone with my children? I also wonder this: What would it have felt like not to see yourself in your wife's work? Not to see yourself represented in this expression of the lives of your family?

These are difficult questions for me to ask myself. I told you before: This isn't the story of a good wife and a bad husband. Maybe this is a story of two human beings who committed to each other very young and didn't survive one another's changes.

When I teach and edit, I ask poets to consider what in their poem is essential. What does the reader need? What is the poem insisting upon? When you consistently leave something—or someone—out of your poems, that's a conspicuous absence. In not writing my husband into my poems, did I consider him "nonessential"? It's difficult to answer that now. But I will say this: I felt that he was separate. I felt it was the kids and me, day after day, most of the time. I felt that the fourth member of the family rowed away from our island to work, and then rowed back to us, but we three lived there. That was daily life.

I'm careful to say "I felt," because there is no one truth to be told in this regard. It feels invasive to even consider what it might have felt like to be the one in the boat, oars in both hands. To go away and come back, again and again, and to miss so much living. It is a kind of estrangement, maybe, to be the one who works outside of the home. *Estrangement* as in "to be made strange," to feel apart from.

Now it feels prescient, to use Sonia's term. Maybe it's only possible to travel very far away if one is already used to rowing.

I speak here of poetry as the revelation or distillation of experience. . . .
                                                            —Audre Lorde

BUT HERE'S THE THING

I can't distill what I'm not permitted to fully experience. I can't extract meaning from what's being withheld from me, kept secret, buried.

How do I distill the silence, the knowing that I don't know?

A NOTE ON BETRAYAL

Yes, I'm still thinking about betrayal. *Ruminating* is what my therapist would call it. *Rumination* makes me think of cows and their extra stomachs. Their *fermenting* stomachs. It makes me think of myself as a ruminant, a human variation, except the fermentation happens where? The head. The chest. How in my mind and my heart, I can chew and chew on a thing and never swallow it.

Okay, enough about cows.

Betrayal is neat because it preempts me from having to look, *really* look, at my marriage. Toward the end, my husband and I were distant, and the distance makes sense. If you feel that someone is being unkind or unfair to you, you don't want to be close to them. Then you aren't close to them, so you grow further apart. More unkindness, more distance. It's a vicious cycle, and breaking it requires deep work.

I'll never know what might have happened, what work might have been possible, and who we would have been, individually and together, on the other side of that work. I'll never know if I'd outgrown the relationship or just the dynamic between us. With work, would that dynamic have shifted?

Betrayal is neat because it creates a diversion. When there's an explosion on one side of the street, no one is looking at the other side. You can easily just slip away in the commotion. Maybe we slipped away in the commotion. I need to chew on that some more.

CLUES TO THE MYSTERY

I keep trying to make sense of our history—*make* a strange verb for it, as if sense is something to be fashioned, and from what? Notions of the truth, or time, or experience? I'm trying to retrace my steps, to follow the bread-crumb trail back to *before*, back to when I believe he loved me and was proud of me, back to when I believe we were happy. I'm trying to see where the cracks in our life started. More than anything, I want to understand. I'm seeking The Pattern, as I tried with my newborn son, writing everything down, as if I could solve him.

"What happened?" people ask, as if recounting events makes—*assembles*—sense. There is what happened—*plot*—and then there is what the book is about. There is what happened, and then there is the meaning we tease from it.

Spoiler Alert: I still haven't solved the mystery. Not all of it. Where is that omniscient narrator when we need her most?

A FRIEND SAYS EVERY BOOK BEGINS WITH AN UNANSWERABLE QUESTION

Then what is mine?
where did it go

PLEASE DON'T

It was March, three months before I reached my hand into my husband's work bag and pulled out a postcard. I was attending the AWP conference in Tampa, Florida, with thousands of other writers and editors. *Good Bones* had come out the previous October, so I had three full days of panels, readings, and book signings scheduled.

My friend Ann was there, and her husband, who was my husband's colleague at the time, had come to the conference with her. I loved seeing the two of them at the firm's Christmas parties and summer parties—and I loved that I wasn't the only poet spouse. At the conference, Ann's husband walked up as I was signing copies of *Good Bones* in the book fair: "Let me take a picture of your signing line and send it to him."

"Please don't," I said. "It'll just make everything worse."

I was having a good time—it was work, but I enjoyed it. And he was home doing *my* work. To be fair, I treated it that way, too. I had internalized that. He was "covering for me," as if I were a coworker who'd gone on vacation and left my cubicle-neighbor with all my tasks while I was away. I should be thankful—and I *was* thankful! I should feel bad—and I *did* feel bad! I felt bad because I saw other women with spouses and kids, and their husbands picked up the phone with a warm "Hi, how's it going?" They asked about their wives' panel discussions, readings, signings. They put the children on the phone, then asked for the phone back to say "I love you!" before they hung up. Some of the husbands even came along. I envied that. I wanted what they had.

THE SPREADSHEET

One afternoon while the kids were at school, I was cleaning the house, listening to an episode of Nora McInerny's podcast, *Terrible, Thanks For Asking*. Her guest, Eve Rodsky, told a story about being on a trip with several close friends when everyone's husbands were calling or texting. *Where were the snacks? Did they need a birthday present for the party? What time was soccer?* Instead of staying overnight on that trip as planned, many of her friends went home, because it was easier to do the work themselves—finding the snacks, getting the gift, managing soccer—than to walk their husbands through doing it, or to deal with anxious calls or snarky texts.

She came back from her trip and started to make a spreadsheet of all the tasks that were her responsibility in her marriage—all the things on her plate, big and small. It ended up growing into a massive spreadsheet, which she emailed to her husband as a way of opening up a conversation about the division of labor in their home.

I can't do that. It's too late to do anything about the inequity in my now-kaput marriage. But I made the list of tasks anyway. I wanted to see in black and white what I'd been doing in the marriage. Reader, I was going to show you the list, but I decided against it. You don't need the list.

Looking at it, I thought, *No wonder so many divorced men get remarried right away and so many divorced women stay on their own.* I saw something I'm still trying to process: My life looked surprisingly like my mother's. My mother didn't go to college, married at twenty, and had me at twenty-four. I went to college and graduate school, published my first book and got married at twenty-eight (at which age she already had three children), and had my children in my thirties. Still, *still*, my life looked a lot like hers.

I don't say this with frustration because my mother's life isn't a good, beautiful life—it is! If you ask her, she'll tell you she wanted to be a mother more than anything else in the world. That's what she wanted to be when she grew up: a mom. No, I say this with frustration because I saw myself and my husband as different—more progressive, more equal in our household, both with graduate degrees, both respected in our fields—but were we? The division of labor in our home told a different story. I was angry at myself, and more than a little ashamed, that I allowed this to happen, and that I had unwittingly modeled to Violet and Rhett what women's work was—the baking of class Valentine's treats, the pairing of socks, the buying and wrapping of gifts, the packing of school lunches and camp snacks, the applying of sunscreen. Caregiving.

Did my children see their father's job as more "real" than mine because it happened outside the home, and because despite my work, I was the primary caregiver? I felt that he treated my (writing) work like an interruption of my (domestic) work, and did they see that, too? When I traveled, I planned carefully for minimal disruption to his schedule. I arranged playdates for after school or asked my parents for help. But I couldn't pack lunches ahead, give baths ahead, make breakfasts ahead, get the kids dressed ahead, anticipate fevers or stomach flus ahead. Some things would have to be done in real time.

When my husband traveled for work, I looked forward to his return—especially if the kids were sick or I had multiple deadlines of my own—but the daily fires were ones I was used to putting out myself. On the other hand, when I would call home from a trip, I remember feeling like I was in trouble. I'd made his life more difficult, and I might pay for that with the silent treatment or a cold reception when I returned home. No *how was your trip?* No *congratulations* or *glad it went well* or *I missed you.*

I didn't feel missed as a person, I felt missed as staff. My invisible labor was made painfully visible when I left the house. I was needed back in my post.

ON SECOND THOUGHT

Reader, I posed a question: Did my children see their father's job as more "real" than mine because it happened outside the home, and because I was the primary caregiver? I suspect the answer is *yes*. And honestly, that perception might endure.

But here's something I've come to terms with since the divorce: *I* treated my husband's job as more "real," more important, than mine, too. He was the primary breadwinner. His work paid our living expenses and provided our family's health insurance. Financially, we could have managed without my income, but we couldn't have managed without his.

Reader, tell me: When one person out-earns another in a marriage, is an imbalance of power inevitable? Is the spouse who earns less expected to take on more of the domestic labor? Is that the deal, spoken or unspoken?

Marriages are cocreated. Whatever ours looked like, we built that together. We inherited parts of it, too.

BRUISES

Rhett is in surgery now. I was just back there singing his favorite songs—
"Graceland," "This Land Is Your Land," "Here Comes the Sun"—and try-
ing not to cry. Now I'm in the waiting room trying to keep it together. Please
send prayers, good juju, and positive thoughts his way. He's my baby.

I posted this on social media the day my son had surgery to address his chronic ear infections—tonsils and adenoids removed, plus tubes implanted in both ears.

It was May. Rhett was five. He had to miss the Mother's Day tea party at preschool because of the surgery, so we had our own tea party on a picnic blanket in the front yard. I got out the fancy teacups and saucers my husband's aunt and uncle had sent from Poland, one covered in golden sunflowers, the other in red poppies. I have some photos from that day—one of Rhett on the blanket, holding his stuffed penguin, and a few shots the next-door neighbor kindly took of the two of us smiling and holding our teacups.

A few days later, Rhett suddenly started bruising all over his legs. First they were small red spots, like a rash, but they grew larger and more bruise-like. He also complained that he hurt, all over. After an appointment with the pediatrician and an ER visit, he was diagnosed with vasculitis—Henoch-Schönlein Purpura, or HSP. The symptoms are severe joint pain and purpura rash all over from the waist down. There's no treatment other than pain management, and an episode usually lasts two to four weeks. None of this was good news, except it was incredible news, because vasculitis wasn't the worst-case scenario film I had playing in my head when I saw the bruises but hadn't yet seen his lab results. It wasn't leukemia. My boy would be okay.

Still, the bruising was caused by blood vessels bursting, and we were advised to keep an eye out for more severe symptoms. One morning he woke with blood in his underwear, crying for me. *Mom, mom, mom.* Back to the ER. The burst veins were causing some internal bleeding.

A couple of weeks later, my husband pulled into the driveway after work in a black luxury sedan, not the red hatchback he'd left the house in that morning. He was wearing new prescription aviator sunglasses. I half-jokingly tweeted a poll: *Is he having a midlife crisis?* The answer choices were *yes* or *gurl yesssssss.*

Gurl yesssssss won with 76 percent of the votes. One of the comments: *He has a new gf.*

I laughed about that, because of course he didn't. A week later, I found the postcard.

How I picture it: That life was a boat. I could almost hear the water slapping at the sides of it. I felt the floor moving beneath me as if rising and falling on waves.

It was an illusion: I was on land. I was in Ohio, and there were trees outside—our neighbor's magnolias, and the many sycamores lining Roosevelt Avenue, with their peeling, paint-by-number bark, and the occasional maple or oak or Bradford pear. There were pines, too, and some of them dropped what looked like small wooden grenades on the ground.

My legs weren't used to standing. My head swam.

IN THE BEGINNING

In the beginning I told no one about the pinecone, the postcard, the notebook. I wanted to save my marriage, but I wanted to save it without anyone knowing it needed saving.

That is some serious firstborn-daughter energy right there.

First I confided in one of my sisters. Next I reached out to Jen, my dear friend for more than twenty years and my neighbor a block away. Jen, who also happens to be a child psychologist.

I met her for dinner that week at Giuseppe's, a family-owned Italian restaurant in our neighborhood, and sitting at a two-top near the bar, I told her everything: what I'd found, what he'd said, what he didn't know I knew. She was as incredulous and pissed off and loving as I needed her to be. Who brings their son a souvenir from a walk with another woman? Who surgically removes pages from a notebook?

In other words: How did he *do* that?

She recommended a couples counselor walkable from my house. When I brought it up with my husband—maybe therapy could help us get through this—he agreed to go, so I emailed the woman to set up an appointment. In the meantime, as everything was unraveling, I leaned on Jen, Lisa, Kelly, Ann, Victoria, Wendy, Dawn. (Thank god for the saving grace of friendship, and especially the friendship of other wives and mothers. Thank god for happy hours and long walks and phone calls and texts.) I leaned on my sisters, Katie and Carly, too, but it would be months before I told my mother. I thought I could fix it, and she'd never have to know, as if I were a teenager again, and I'd broken a vase while she was on vacation. As if I could just glue it back together before she returned. I was protecting him, and more than that, protecting their relationship. So I worked quietly, in secret, to save my marriage. I worked quietly to fix it so no one would know it was—*we* were—broken.

PINECONE

This is what Jen's husband calls The Addressee. *Pinecone*.

CRYING ON THE COUCH

My husband and I sat side by side on a couch in the marriage counselor's office. It was a love seat, actually. A *love seat* of all things. To my right, my husband. To my left, a box of tissues on the side table, which I remember well because I pulled tissue after tissue from that box, week after week. Outside the office door, a white noise machine—the exact same one our children had in each of their bedrooms—helped mask the conversations happening inside.

We started counseling about a month after I found the postcard. Our sessions were usually on my husband's lunch hour, so we met at the counselor's office. Eventually, without saying a word about it, she began to cushion our appointments with an extra half hour after he left to drive back to work. She could see I needed more time to stop crying and calm down enough to leave. I worried about being seen there, because the building was so close to our home, and because there were other businesses inside. What if we saw someone we knew?

I didn't tell the counselor about the postcard or the notebook, as if not saying it aloud could keep it in the realm of the not-quite-real. As if the moment I told her, it would become true. The Addressee wasn't the problem, after all, right? She was a symptom. So what was the problem? My work was the problem. *I* was the problem—my traveling for readings, workshops, conferences. That wasn't the deal, though I didn't know we'd had a deal.

THE PLAY

The Finder has lost her narrative, but the play continues. In this scene, imagine that she sits beside The Husband on The Marriage Counselor's love seat. They talk about the problem: The Finder's work travel. Her work. Her.

It's in the stage directions: her hot frustration and sadness; his coolness.

Maybe The Husband is unhappy that the children see The Wife on her laptop and on her phone. The Finder is always working, and the children see it.

"The kids don't see you work because you go to an office all day," The Finder says. "If I had an office to go to every day, the kids wouldn't see me working much either."

The Finder is self-employed. There is no company, no firm. She has no one to delegate to. But she points out that she works fewer hours than her husband. She doesn't have billable hours, after all. Time isn't money in the same way. But isn't her time still valuable?

In this scene, The Marriage Counselor says, "Travel is an expectation of your job. You wouldn't tell your employer, 'No, I can't do that.' Don't you think that travel is also an expectation of her job? Isn't that something publishers expect of authors?"

The lighting designer knows what to do here. The Finder glows faintly red; The Husband, blue. The set designer made sure to place the box of tissues beside The Finder, and she reaches for one. The white noise machine whirs just outside the door, as if they're newborns who need to be lulled to sleep. Sometimes The Finder feels like a newborn, pulled out of some comfortable known space into . . . what exactly?

A NOTE ON CONFLICT & CRISIS

unny how much easier it is to write my life in third person. To write *she* instead of *I*, *hers* instead of *mine*. Funny how much easier it is to write through the lens of plot and character and setting and inciting incident and conflict and crisis—to feel that sense of remove.

It was not a play, not a novel, not a film. It was—*is*—my life.

Being a freelancer and a primary caregiver isn't glamorous. Most of the time I'm at home, cobbling together a living—writing, editing manuscripts for other poets, teaching online. Packing lunches, planning meals, grocery shopping. Walking the dog. Moving the wet laundry to the dryer. Moving the dirty dishes to the dishwasher. Sending and answering emails. Folding the clean, dry laundry, and leaving a new stack on each child's bed. Walking the dog again. Sending and answering more emails, emails, emails. Emptying the dishwasher before the dishes have cooled, and letting them burn my fingertips.

Arguably, being the primary breadwinner is no more glamorous than being the primary caregiver. My husband went to work each day, all day, and sometimes had commitments on weekends and in the evenings. He had business travel, too. He didn't need permission to do his work. He didn't have to ask me to "cover for him" while he worked, since that is precisely what I'd done all along. When he traveled, there was never a question of "Can I go now?" or "Can you manage without me?" It was a given.

When Rhett was a newborn, my husband took a position as board president of a local arts organization. I remember saying, "Really? Now?" Or did I only think that? Did I say nothing? It doesn't matter now. That was that. The decision was made. Of course I would be home, and of course I would manage.

That was, apparently, the deal.

My occasional travel had been a sore spot in our marriage since before "Good Bones" went viral, but more and more requests were coming in to my speakers agency because of that poem. I'd spend two days here, four days there, and a couple of times a year I'd be gone for a weeklong workshop, but the bulk of my time was spent at home. I'd work while the kids were at daycare and school, and again after they went to bed at night. I was a stay-at-home (or, rather, work-from-home) mom who traveled occasionally. So what? I'd been self-employed since Violet was two, and even before then, I'd been the one to take off work when she was sick, to take her to scheduled appointments, to hire childcare and schedule summer camp. I did the same for Rhett. I managed my own schedule and the children's schedules.

An invitation to give a reading or attend a conference or book festival meant I wouldn't be available. Even if I arranged after-school playdates for the kids, even if I planned for my parents to be available until he arrived home from work, who would pack the school lunches? Who would drop them off in the morning? Who was going to make sure the favorite pajamas were clean for "PJ and Stuffy Day" at school? And—always a fear—what if one of them ran a fever and couldn't go to school? This was "extra work" for him—and extra emotional labor, too—because, as the self-employed parent, I'd always handled these things. And, meanwhile, what would I be doing for work? Reading poems, teaching workshops, going to dinners, giving talks, being interviewed in front of an audience? Maybe for business it sure sounded a lot like pleasure?

Once, while I was at a literary festival in Spokane, my husband called from Ohio: I needed to come home right away. Rhett had a fever. I wouldn't have made this call to him if he'd been traveling for business. I wouldn't have expected him to cancel work engagements and fly home across the country because of a fever. If I needed help with the kids, I would have called my parents, my sisters, my friends. By the time I got home, my son was fine. His fever was gone, but the house was hot with anger.

Remember, I asked you to dog-ear this earlier: We became friends in a creative writing workshop. When I got good news related to my writing—a publication, a grant, an invitation—I sensed him wince inwardly. So I stopped sharing good news. I made myself small, folded myself up origami tight. I canceled or declined upcoming events: *See, I'll do anything to make this marriage work.* I gave up income and professional opportunities, but those sacrifices didn't save my marriage.

We were both busy, probably spread too thin, needing things from our lives—and from one another—that we weren't getting. I agreed that something needed to give. I disagreed that the something needed to be my work. In turn, me.

What would I have done to save my marriage? I would have abandoned myself, and I did, for a time. I would have done it for longer if he'd let me.

THE MATERIAL

The question I keep asking myself as I write this book, the question I keep insisting upon, is this: How can this story—this experience—be useful to anyone other than me? How can I make this material into a tool you can use?

To talk back to myself: experience is instructive. People make connections on their own. When I make a metaphor, I offer the comparison, but the distance between vehicle and tenor is distance the reader must cross. I can't carry you from one to the other. I can't carry you from the nesting doll to the self, or from the boat to the life—you have to get yourself there.

I need to trust that I can hand this to you, just as it is, and it will mean something to you. I need to trust that you'll know what to do with it.

Here, take it. Is this enough? This is my material.

THE LAST FAMILY VACATION

t was August, which is always miserably hot and humid—and sometimes volatile and stormy—in Ohio. My husband and I had been in marriage counseling for a month, me crying on the love seat each week while he sat beside me. I'd been sleeping in our bed, and he'd been sleeping on the couch. But we'd planned and paid for a summer beach trip the previous year, so we packed up the SUV, strapped the hot-pink ThunderShirt around our anxious dog, hoping it would help her stay calm on the long drive, and we hit the road.

I'd packed my sadness, despite its enormous size. Each day I lugged it down to the beach with my towel and beach chair and sunglasses and paperback and sunblock and water bottle.

Every shell I handed Rhett, he threw into the surf—for someone else to find, he said—while Violet rinsed each one and dropped it into the pail of "keepers." The sea isn't discerning in what it keeps, what it discards. *Discards* feels more like *delivers* when you're standing on the beach, all those broken pieces left at your feet: shards of abalone, tiger-striped spines of conch, gray wedges of sand dollar, none from the same whole. Like the mismatched dishes we cobbled from our mothers' cupboards in the early years, some from their 1970s weddings—the brown crockware from my childhood, the green-flowered white melamine from my husband's.

There were so few things intact—a few spirals, a handful of bead-small snail shells, and the copper-peach coins, pearlescent and penny-sized. They glinted up at us from the sand. I slipped them, still gritty, into my pockets. We kept what we wanted, and what we didn't, the tide hauled away.

During that last family vacation, I stayed on the deck or in our rented beach house most of the time, because my grief was such a heavy thing to carry to the water. Sand is hard enough to walk in, all resistance. It pulls you down, swallows you up to your ankles.

A couple of days into the trip, lying in bed late at night with my back to my husband, I broke. I started crying, then wrapped myself in a light cotton blanket and walked out onto the back deck. He followed me outside.

I sat in the deck chair and sobbed, listening to the ocean waves though it was too dark to see them. I remember the wind and so many stars, unmoved by the wind. I must have looked like a small child, wearing pajamas, my knees pulled up to my chin, blanket wrapped around me. I remember saying "I want my mom" and "I want to go home." But of course going home was impractical. We had driven more than ten hours over the course of two days with our children and the dog. We had one car there. One of us could fly home alone, but what would we tell the kids? We hadn't told them anything yet. Nothing.

It was too much to even think about. I was too exhausted, too sad, to make those kinds of plans. So I stayed, and I wrote. Violet didn't love being down at the beach for long—she preferred reading books in the air-conditioning—so she and I stuck close to the house most days with the dog, moving between the sunny deck overlooking the ocean and the living room, while "the boys," as we called them, spent time in the water. For the rest of the week, my husband and I were rarely together, and when we were, we spoke to the children instead of one another.

On the long drive home, I sat in a Circle K parking lot, waiting in the car with Violet and the dog for my husband to get back from the bathroom with Rhett. I looked up to see them walking toward us hand in hand across the parking lot. Even though we weren't speaking, even though he didn't smile at me, I chose then to smile at him, to use my bright voice—because my antidepressants were working, and the sky was delft and cloudless, and our son's hair was a nest of yellow straw from a week at the sea. I was ashamed to think of how I'd leashed my joy and tugged hard every time it tried to run.

IT ISN'T ABOUT THE WAVES

Back in counseling when we got home, the topic was our trip. His narrative: We had gone to the beach with our kids, and I never played in the waves. My perspective: Never was hyperbole. Rarely is true.

What I said: "I didn't want to be near him. I was too sad."

What I didn't say: I thought about dying all the time. Or, not dying, but disappearing. *Poof.* I didn't want to die, not really, but I wanted relief. I wanted to stop feeling what I was feeling. I carried all of that with me to the coast, and I didn't know what to do with it there.

The sticking point: I wrote poems at the ocean and didn't play in the waves.

The marriage counselor said, "It isn't about the waves."

What I said: "He knows I've never liked being in the ocean much. Even before we had kids, I mostly sat in my beach chair and read or wrote."

What I didn't say: The thing about the ocean is I don't feel safe in it, because I can't see what's in there with me. I know I'm not alone in the water, but I don't know what's there.

What I didn't say: I wrote poems at the beach because I needed to make something more than sadness.

What I didn't say: I'm adding my sadness to the list of things we'll never get the sand out of. Like anything you take to the beach, it'll be gritty forever.

THE WATER

One night a few weeks after the last family vacation, my husband and I had an explosive argument. The kids were in bed, as they always were when we argued. The dynamic was familiar by then: I was wild with emotion; he was hard, distant, sarcastic.

He was propped up on the couch with his pillow and blanket, getting ready to sleep there as he had for more than a month. There was an orange plastic tumbler full of water on the coffee table beside him. In frustration, I picked up the cup and threw it in his direction, dousing him, the couch, his pillow, and the blanket with cold water. I think I shouted "You deserved that!" on my way upstairs. If I didn't say it, I thought it.

Was this my proudest moment? No. I was not my best self that night. I gave all the fucks, I thought. Why was I the one giving all the fucks? Where were *his* fucks?

In our next session, the marriage counselor prompted me to turn to my husband beside me on the couch and apologize. I did. I said, "I'm sorry I threw the cup of water." I stopped myself from adding, "I'm sorry if my anger scares you!"

I wasn't sorry.

How I picture it: For months, maybe even years, I folded and folded my happiness until I couldn't fold it anymore, until it fit under my tongue, and I held it there.

I kept silent in order to hold it.

I taught myself to read his face and dim mine, a good mirror.

TAKING DOWN THE PICTURES

After the night I threw the cup of water, things got . . . worse. We were still living together, but we weren't speaking. He didn't acknowledge my presence. I remember him kissing the kids goodbye before going to work, and it was like I wasn't in the room. Like I was a ghost in my own home. Invisible.

One night, I sat down on our couch, faced him, and finally admitted to reading the notebook before he'd removed the pages. I finally admitted to knowing more than I'd claimed to know. Playing dumb is difficult, and I'd been doing it for months.

I don't know what I expected his reaction to be, but it was anger. Anger and blame. He knew I would react this way. He knew I wouldn't understand. There's a term for this—for when you tell someone they didn't see what they saw, don't know what they know. I'm not using it here.

Another night, in the middle of an intense argument, he went for a walk and wouldn't come back. I kept texting and calling, but he wouldn't respond. I begged him to come home and talk. Who knows who he was talking to, walking the streets of the neighborhood I still live in, the streets I still walk with my children and my dog, but when he came back, I'd taken down all of the pictures of him in our house—off the walls, off the mantel—and put them in the basement. It was completely illogical: as if part of me wanted him back, and part of me wanted him to disappear, and nothing in between would do. Or: I wanted my husband back, and I wanted the stranger he'd become to disappear.

Later that night I put the pictures back up, not because I was sorry, and not because I wanted to see us together, smiling, a seemingly happy and intact family, but because we hadn't told the kids yet. I knew they'd notice the family photos and wedding photos missing, and they'd ask about it. And what would I say?

SOMETHING LIKE RELIEF

I was sitting on the left side of the couch—fine, the *love seat*—looking at the marriage counselor, sensing my husband's tense presence to my right. I summoned my courage.

"I've been thinking, and I need to say something." Deep breath. "Why has this been all about him? What makes *him* happy. What *he* needs. What about what *I* need to be happy?"

I can't be certain, but I swear I saw something like relief on the counselor's face.

Looking back on that afternoon, I put myself in her shoes. What would it be like to have a couple come in to see me, and their immediate crisis is this: the man doesn't want the woman to continue traveling for her work, but he's going to keep traveling for his. What would it be like to watch the woman frantically agree to try to appease her husband? Would this imbalance of power trouble me? Would I expect their "plan" to fail? If the answers are yes and yes, then a look of relief would make sense, but I'll never be sure.

That day in the marriage counselor's office, I came clean. I finally told her about the postcard, the notebook, The Addressee. I finally admitted to myself what I'd been trying to avoid: I couldn't be the person—or the writer, or the mother—I wanted to be in my marriage. The "deal" wasn't working.

Walking home from our last counseling session, I knew. We'd separate, definitely. Divorce, maybe. He'd get his own place, at least for a while. We'd have the family talk that breaks kids' hearts.

I'd been trying to save the marriage, but I needed to save myself.

A NOTE ON PLOT

O r maybe this isn't a note about plot at all. This isn't about what happened but about what it *means*.

One day, it hit me: The best things to happen to me individually were the worst things to happen to my marriage.

And then, this: But the best things remain.

SOME PEOPLE ASK

"Was it always like this?"

There's a cost to answering fully. There's a cost to carving out a partial response.

—I could say that of the things that chipped away at us as a couple—having children, the demands of his career, the demands of mine—maybe one of the three would've been survivable. But all of them together? I could say that the hairline fractures created by parenting and working, by suffering in ways seen and unseen, by sacrificing, began to grow into larger cracks. I think one crack joined another, which joined another, until the whole thing split wide open. I could say that we became friends in a creative writing workshop. I think that fact communicates some of the tension in our marriage, particularly in the last years. I could say that he could travel and did—that's how he met The Addressee, after all—so it was only fair that I could travel, too. When he left town for work, it was just part of his job, and I expected my travel to be treated the same. It wasn't the same. I could say that when I worked full-time in publishing, my boss wouldn't allow me to take time off for my writing—not even unpaid time. Again, in my marriage, I felt that I needed permission, authorization, to clock out, log off, hand the work to someone else for a few days. "Can you cover for me?" suggests it is your work to do, not a shared responsibility. I could quote my friend Jen, who says the work she does makes her husband's life possible. I could talk about invisible labor—how there are gears turning inside the machine that no one sees, but if they stop turning the whole thing grinds to a smoking halt. I could talk about the expectation of how I would spend my time: caregiving was my primary work and my career was secondary, whereas for him it was the opposite. I could say that we both built that, we'd done that together, but it was working for one of us, so only one of us wanted to dismantle it—

"No, it wasn't always like this, not exactly. And yes, in some ways, it was." Next question.

BANK LOLLIPOPS

I was standing in our downstairs bathroom the minute I knew: We were getting divorced.

A few minutes earlier, I'd finally gotten the password to our joint savings account. Friends had been advising me to look at the accounts now that we were having problems, but it didn't seem important to me. When I accessed the savings account, though, I saw that half, exactly half, had been withdrawn right after our last argument. To be clear: I wasn't depositing money in our savings account; I never even looked at it. But I knew it existed for us and our kids, and it was what we drew from for vacations, a new furnace, a car repair.

The kids were home with me, and their father was at work. I shut myself in the tiny downstairs half bath. I had to go into my phone contacts to call him, because we talked so rarely then, he was no longer in my "recents." We were hardly speaking at that point, except in therapy. When he picked up, I could hear from the background noise that he was in his car.

"Did you take half the savings out of our account?"

Yes, he had. His lawyer had advised it.

"Your *lawyer*? You have a lawyer? Like a *divorce* lawyer?"

Yes. He had a divorce lawyer.

I hung up the phone. I didn't have a divorce lawyer. I didn't know until that moment that I needed one.

I panicked. How would I pay for a divorce lawyer? Marriage is an economic institution, and the end of a marriage can spell economic disaster—especially for women, who are more likely to be the primary caregivers and not the primary earners in a household. I didn't know if I had the legal right to withdraw the other half of the savings account, but I figured if his lawyer told him to take exactly half, it was probably because I was entitled to the other half. And now I would need it.

I looked at the clock. Almost 5:00. The bank would be closing. I was crying, but I splashed water on my face, dried it with a hand towel, and walked out of the bathroom and into the kitchen.

"Kids, get your shoes on—we need to run to the bank!" It was pouring outside. "There was a mistake, and I need to go fix it."

We drove to our small bank branch just a block away, and I said I'd run in and would be right back. They knew to expect a lollipop, because that was a pleasure of going to the bank with Mom.

I ran inside and walked up to the counter. I could see my parked car through the large lobby windows, my children inside, playing games on their tablets. I knew the teller—I'd been in several times a month to deposit checks. I'd obviously been crying, and he looked at me with concern.

"Is there something I can help you with?" he asked.

I leaned in and whispered across the counter to him. "I just found out my husband took half of our savings and moved it to a new account, and I need the other half. Can you help me?"

"I'm so sorry. Yes, I can help." In just a few clicks, he moved the other half of our joint savings account to the business account I used for freelance work, which was in my name only. I looked around the counter.

"Is there something else you need, ma'am?" he asked.

"Where are the suckers? They're usually up here." I sniffled, fighting back more tears.

He smiled and motioned to the table where the deposit slips and pens were kept. "Oh, we moved them."

I grabbed three—one for each of us. "I'm taking three!" I called back to him on my way out, forcing a smile. "We deserve these!"

Because if you've just found out your marriage is over, you should at least get a sucker. Root beer, maybe. Or butterscotch.

That night, I emailed a lawyer.

How I picture it: Marriages are nesting dolls, too.

We carry each iteration: the marriage we had before the children, the marriage of love letters and late nights at dive bars and train rides through France; the marriage we had after the children, the marriage of tenderness but transactional communication—who's doing what, and when, and how—and early mornings and stroller walks and crayon on the walls and sunscreen that always needs to be reapplied; the marriage we had toward the end before we knew there was an end, the marriage of the silent treatment and couch sleeping and the occasional update email.

Somewhere at the center is the tiniest doll. Love. The love that started everything. It's still there, but we'd have to open and open and open ourselves—our together selves—to find it.

I can't bear to think of it in there somewhere, the love. Like the perfect pit of some otherwise rotten fruit.

For to wish to forget how much you loved someone—and then to actually forget—can feel, at times, like the slaughter of a beautiful bird who chose, by nothing short of grace, to make a habitat of your heart.

—Maggie Nelson

GROUNDS

On the divorce paperwork, you have to list a reason. There is no box to check next to viral poem or thrown cup of water or pinecone or billable hours or miscarriages or work travel or postcard or stowaway or depression or ultimatums or excised notebook pages or creative frustration or daycare drop-offs or silent treatment. *Irreconcilable differences* didn't cover it—I could see a pages-long parenthetical after the term, a list of what had happened, a list of clues in a mystery I could not and will not solve. But the term would have to do.

THIS MOMENT ISN'T FOR YOU

Reader, I'm not going to give you a scene of us telling our kids we were getting divorced. I won't tell you what we said, and I won't tell you how they reacted. It was the hardest conversation I've ever had with anyone, period. I hope to never have one harder.

That moment their lives were changed forever, and that moment isn't for you. I'm not going to tell you about how they coped then or how they're coping now, as I write this. That story is theirs to tell how and when they wish, or not to tell at all.

I don't have all the answers—there is no manual for how to do this—but I do know this: I will guard my kids like Fort Fucking Knox. From everyone. Including myself.

BITTERSWEET

It was October, and my husband was still living in our house, though the children knew he'd be moving out soon. He'd said something about wanting his old life back, as if the past were intact, waiting for us to come back and collect it. But soon Rhett would turn six, and even he knew five was gone, four was gone—or it was somewhere nested inside him, part of him. You carry the past with you, but you can't go back.

Maybe when we long for our "old lives" in middle age, what we're longing for is our *young* lives. The reprisal of a past role? A curtain call?

We celebrated Rhett's sixth birthday separately that year; at the party, it was me, Rhett, Violet, my parents, my sisters and brothers-in-law, my niece and nephews. I told Rhett he'd have two birthdays from now on—one with his father, one with me—and I'd still bake any cake he asks for. The year before it was from-scratch chocolate and vanilla buttercream, topped with maraschino cherries and rainbow sprinkles. For his sixth, he wanted chocolate cheesecake, the one I always make from Alice Medrich's *Bittersweet* cookbook.

Bittersweet. I couldn't make this up.

There were candles. And before I struck the match, there was singing.

KEEP MOVING

A few days after my son turned six, I wrote myself a note and shared it on social media: *Do not be stilled by anger or grief. Burn them both and use that fuel to keep moving. Look up at the clouds and tip your head way back so the roofs of the houses disappear. Keep moving.*

I had no idea at the time, but this would become a daily practice. Later, it would become a book.

GHOST STORY

That fall I was a ghost in my own house. That fall, when divorce was imminent but my husband and I were still living together, only the children could see or hear me. The laundry floated downstairs to the basement, then floated back up to the second floor, washed and folded. The dishes floated from the dishwasher and into the cabinets, chiming as they nested inside each other. I floated through the house, practically transparent. Maybe my perfume stayed behind when I left a room. I tried to rattle my chains, but what chains?

I half wanted to be a ghost. I remember thinking, then telling a friend: *I want to cut a hole in the air and climb inside.*

LUCKY THIRTEEN

I spent the morning of my thirteenth wedding anniversary in my lawyer's office. "Lucky thirteen." I laughed ruefully, because if you don't laugh . . .

I was sitting in a conference room just off the lobby, my lawyer across the table sliding me paperwork to sign, when my phone started ringing in my purse. I checked it—when you have kids you always check—and saw the name. Jim. *Oof*. My dear friend Jim, who'd been at our wedding, called every year on our anniversary. I let it go to voicemail.

I was there to finalize the shared parenting plan. Not having this paperwork done was the one thing that was keeping my husband from moving out of our home, so I was eager to get it signed and filed. Living together for the month prior was easily the worst month of my life. I hadn't even told anyone about the divorce except close friends and family. I don't know who he'd told at that point—and, maybe more importantly, what he'd told them. I didn't know what his narrative was until fairly recently, when an old friend of ours reached out and we finally spoke. It had been years. As it turns out, his narrative was pretty much what I expected. Funny how people remain predictable in some ways even when they're able to shock you in others.

When I left my lawyer's office that morning, I sat in my car in the parking lot and listened to Jim's message. "Congratulations!" he said. "Lucky thirteen! To get this far and with two beautiful kids takes a lot of hard work. You did it!"

There have been times in my life when I felt like I was in an indie movie, and I could feel the audience cringing at the scene. The "happy anniversary" call received in the attorney's office was one of those times. I could almost see myself as if filmed from the adjacent parking spot—look at that woman, sitting in her car, her phone to her ear. Watch her grimace, check her hair in the visor mirror, find a song she can turn way up with the sunroof open. Watch her reverse, then pull out of the parking lot onto the street. She looks like someone who is used to the sea and is now on dry land.

I didn't have the heart to call him back. I emailed him later that day, explaining: *Jim, thank you so much for your message. Forgive the email response but I didn't think I could keep it together on the phone. I was in my lawyer's office when you called. [Redacted] and I are divorcing. Not my choice, but I'm coming to terms with it. It's been brutal, but I have a great support system, you included. Big love to you. xoxo M*

My husband would move out a couple of weeks later. What I didn't know: We'd still be married the next year, on our fourteenth anniversary, because the divorce wouldn't be finalized yet. The first anniversary we would be officially untethered, the first former wedding anniversary, would be our fifteenth, twenty years after we moved into our first apartment together, full of hope as all people in love in their early twenties are. The sails were full of wind and the sun was shining, and there was nothing in the water below the boat, nothing that could harm us.

UPDATING AND UNBLURRING

It was November when my husband moved out of our house and into a rental house several blocks away, marking the end of our nearly nineteen-year relationship, but Google Maps didn't notice. That morning I had whisked the children away so he and two friends from law school could load his things into a U-Haul and drive to the house he had rented.

We had agreed that he would be the one to move out, and we agreed on what he would take: the dining room set and painting that had belonged to his late boss; the sideboards we had bought to hold our wedding dishes; and the antique armoire a neighbor in our first apartment complex had left us because it wouldn't fit in his moving truck.

I had packed most of his things because he works long hours. I had sifted through our books and CDs, our Christmas ornaments, our coffee mugs. The blender: his. The food processor: mine. The biscuit cutter: his. The muffin tin: mine. The life we had lived, split between us.

It was more than a month before I even saw the house he moved to, though it was only a few blocks away.

In early December, a few weeks after he moved, I was on a writing residency in Tucson, far from my home in Ohio. I'm not sure what possessed me to Google our address from the desert, but I did, and there it was: my house on Google Maps, my husband still inside. And still, I thought, in love with me. The photo was dated January 2016.

No, it was daylight in the photo, so he was at work. The blue recycling bins were at the curb, full, so I knew it was a Monday morning. There was light snow on the ground, and my neighbor's magnolia trees were bare. They bloom in the spring and are impossibly beautiful for a few days, and then the blossoms drop and make a mess of both our yards.

I love them anyway.

Even though it was winter, my son's tricycle was on the front porch. This is what passes as bike storage when you don't have a garage. The snow shovel was probably propped nearby, too. I couldn't zoom in enough to see the yellow bag of sidewalk salt by the front door, but I knew it was there. I knew the orange plastic tumbler was nestled inside it, a makeshift scoop.

I was probably inside, alone; my husband would be home in the evening. I was likely working on my laptop, clacking away with my index fingers because I never learned how to type, not properly. Maybe I was reheating the cup of coffee I always let go cold.

In the afternoon, once the recycling had been picked up, I'd retrieve the cracked bins from the driveway and haul them back to the side of the house. I'd walk to pick up my daughter from the elementary school. She and I would drive together to fetch my son from daycare.

The scene could not have been more different from Tucson, where the landscape was red and rocky, another planet, with more stars in the sky than I had seen anywhere.

On my laptop screen I could see the windows of my house, the door, the periwinkle siding and the poor excuse for a flower bed—really just a moat of mulch. I could see the front walk my husband will come up in his suit and overcoat. It would be around 6:00 in the evening, already dark. The children and I might have seen him through the storm door, and my son, only three in January 2016, might have yelled "Daddy!" and run to greet him.

That cold winter morning, someone from Google drove by and took that photo. Two and a half years later, my marriage became untenable.

In the version of my house that still exists online, January 2016, I couldn't see the pairs of my husband's shoes piled under the dining room table or his teacups forgotten around the house, brown-ringed, but I knew they were there. The books he was reading then—so many books at once—were stacked by the old recliner, the one in which we rocked our son countless times.

My husband's shampoo was in the shower, his razor and shaving cream by the sink. His toothbrush and pillow were still upstairs; he didn't begin sleeping on the couch until two summers later, and that version of our house will never be online—the version where we live together but not together.

I saw that people—other people, people like me—had questions for Google Maps: "How do I remove my home image?" "How do I update the picture of my house?" "How do I unblur my house?"

When I looked at my house on Google Maps, I was looking at another life. A blurred life I'm still trying to bring into focus.

"Most photography is done by car," I read, "but some is done by trekker, tricycle, walking, boat, snowmobile and underwater apparatus."

I learned that in 2018, Google Japan began offering the street view from a dog's perspective. But in January 2016, we didn't have a dog. We adopted our Boston terrier at the end of April that year. She had been abused, and her hip bones and spine jutted out from under her marbled coat.

She bit my husband on the hand the day we brought her home, when he tried to pick her up and put her in the car. But then she settled and fell asleep in my lap. When I looked at the photo of my house on that Monday morning, I knew I was there alone, no dog curled up, snoring, beside me. No dog with fur, brindle and white, I could bury my face in and cry. I was inside the house. My husband was still coming home. I had no reason yet to cry for him.

I knew better than to torture myself. I should have closed my laptop, made another cup of tea, watched another impossibly orange sunset. I should have written, which is what I went there to do. But I couldn't help myself. I clicked back through the timeline of previous photos, each an iteration of my married life.

I could see November 2015: My car was in the driveway and I was in the house alone or with my three-year-old son. He was not yet in school, only part-time daycare. The Halloween decorations were still up, the ground littered with dry brown leaves. The pine tree by the front door is smothered in a cotton spiderweb he and the children had stretched across it.

That tree died a year later, and he crudely cut it down.

I clicked again and saw August 2014: My car was in the driveway, my son's stroller was parked on the front walk, and my toddler and I must have been in the house. He was probably napping, or maybe we were stacking his bright wooden blocks on the playroom carpet. My phone was probably charging on the kitchen counter. Maybe it lit up when my husband texted to tell me if he'd be home for dinner or not to wait.

I could see June 2012: My car was in the driveway, and the yard was dappled in sunlight and shadow. The neighbor's magnolia trees were full and green, but it was too late for the blossoms. I was inside, alone or with my daughter, and pregnant, due with a boy that October, after two miscarriages in two years. My husband would come home and empty his pockets on the dining room table, the same table he would load into a U-Haul six years later. Every night there was a little pile of him on the table: business cards, loose change, the engraved money clip I gave him for his birthday.

When I looked at my house on Google Maps—having forgotten about the sunset entirely—I saw our family home. I saw the house my children still draw in their pictures of home, periwinkle crayon for the siding, brown for the door, black squares with pluses for windows. When I zoomed in, I could see the stump of the pine. But I didn't see anything that predicted our marriage ending.

How could I update the image of home in my own mind? How could I unblur it?

"Street view is updated every one to three years," I read.

It had been nearly three years since Google last photographed our street, which meant that someday soon a car would drive by with a camera mounted on its roof to tell me what I already knew: I was alone, trying to update, to unblur.

There would be no men's shoes under the dining room table, no stained teacups. The children may be home, or at school, or at their father's house that day.

In my driveway, there would be one car.

ON SECOND THOUGHT

Maybe this isn't a tell-mine. It's a find-mine. I'm out with lanterns, looking.

A FRIEND SAYS EVERY BOOK BEGINS WITH AN UNANSWERABLE QUESTION

Then what is mine?
what is mine

THE EDITS

That piece you read a few pages back? The one about Google Maps? It was first published in the Modern Love column of the *New York Times*. I emailed the essay to my husband as a courtesy before it was published, and he initially responded without asking for any changes to the piece.

Several days later, my lawyer called. My husband's lawyer had called him, demanding that I pull the piece. I don't even think she'd read it.

Then I received an email from my husband with the same demand. It sounded like it was written by a lawyer, not the human being I'd lived with my entire adult life. Despite the legalese he used, I refused to pull the piece. I knew my rights, and my lawyer had my back.

I gave him, once again, a chance to request changes. This time, he did. His edits on the piece—I'm tempted to put *edits* in air quotes here—were more psychologically revealing than almost anything he said in couples counseling or to me privately. The recycling at the curb became "the recycling my husband took to the curb." The cotton spiderweb stretched across our tree for Halloween became "the spiderweb my husband and children stretched across the tree." He redlined—deleted—that he worked long hours, that I packed his things, that the money clip was a birthday present I gave him, that we had kept our wedding dishes in the dining room cabinets he took when he moved out. Most importantly, he redlined any instance of me crying. The man I'd befriended in a writing workshop tried to delete my grief on the page. Redacting *tears*? That was a new one. I was dumbfounded.

I didn't accept those edits.

Strike that: At first, I accepted many of the edits. But when I sent the piece back to Daniel Jones at the *Times*, the document cluttered with comments and tracked changes, he rightfully questioned them. Didn't they weaken the piece? Didn't some parts no longer make sense? Why would you pack his things for him if he didn't work long hours? Why was his toothbrush in the downstairs bathroom?

In the end, I kept only a few of my husband's suggested edits. Maybe I shouldn't have accepted any of them, but I was trying to keep the peace. Now I think, *What peace?*

I spent more in legal fees defending my right to publish that essay than I was paid for the essay.

And the tears? I stetted the tears.

Tears are a sign of powerlessness, a "woman's weapon." It has been a very long war.
                                                                    —Heather Christle

SAD-ASS DIVORCE DREAMS

Most nights in the beginning, when I hadn't yet accepted that the marriage was over, I sobbed myself to sleep. I worked out what I would tell the kids if I woke them: *I had a bad dream*. And for months, I did. I had sad-ass divorce dreams again and again.

In one, my husband wrapped his arms around me, and I buried my face in his neck. I breathed him in. He smelled like himself in the waking world. Everything was just as it was—the slightest sandpaper of stubble on his throat—except not at all. There was no strain, no anger, only tenderness. Then I woke up.

In another dream, we called off the divorce. The relief was short lived, because then I worried about the poems I'd written about our split, poems forthcoming in journals, poems that said things I couldn't take back. I'd told the truth as I'd known it, but the truth had changed. This, of course, is the nature of truth. Then I woke up.

In another, we were already divorced, but he was about to propose again. We would marry a second time, have a second life together. The kids would be so happy. We were sitting in the front seat of a parked car. The backseat was packed with people—strangers—and we needed privacy for that moment. Before he could pop the question, before he could give me a new ring I wouldn't want—or need—to pawn, I woke up.

Sometimes I'd wake up and forget the divorce had happened. My just-waking self was married, and then it would hit me. I was surprised by how fresh the grief was, every time I remembered.

For months after my husband moved out, my subconscious fed me hope, and then my conscious mind pulled the plate away as soon as I opened my eyes. Or I woke and found the plate empty. There had never been hope on it, not even the smallest portion. Eventually my subconscious stopped offering him to me. Maybe it knew I no longer had the appetite.

How I picture it: In some alternate universe, we are still on the boat, the four of us, no stowaway. In another alternate universe, I am on a different boat with a different partner, different children. In yet another, I am alone on the boat—but the stars, the stars.

In the end, all thinking is if, then. If I'd turned my face from his twenty years ago, then what? I would be living a different life, one just adjacent to this one. I could almost sidle over to it now except it's not there.

If not here, then where? If who I would have been is not who I am, then where is she?

Tonight I wept in the bath, letting the water cool, then got dressed again and walked the neighborhood for an hour in the dark, wet-haired, fragrant. I could hear other couples on their porches, talking and laughing in their gold citronella glow.

If, then—what, where, when? And who? And how?

Block after block, I walked alone except for the one who walks not quite beside me. No, she was somewhere—someone—else.

ABOUT THE BODY

The first month I lived alone in my house, I went to see my doctor. I was still on my husband's health insurance, and his employer required an annual physical in order to continue my coverage. Every December I had to go in to my GP for a checkup—weight, blood pressure, fasting blood glucose, the basics. I was sitting on the examination table, the white paper crinkling underneath me, when my doctor asked, "Anything new this year? Health or life changes?"

"I'm getting divorced," I told him. Knowing me, I probably laughed darkly. I probably made some joke about my life falling apart not being great for my health. This is what I do. I hear myself doing it even now: When I get to the most painful part of the telling, I laugh. I break that part into bits. I laugh through the words I have to say, have to hear myself say, have to let hang in the air.

At the time of the physical, I was on a low dose of Lexapro. I had been on it for postpartum depression when Rhett was just a few months old, but weaned myself off before he turned one. I started on it again after "Good Bones" went viral, feeling overwhelmed and anxious from the attention and the uptick in travel and teaching—the being "on"—that came with the attention.

During the physical, I told my doctor I wanted to stay on the Lexapro for the time being, because the saddest year of your life probably isn't a smart time to wean yourself off an antidepressant. I'm sure I cackled about that, too. My stand-up material was dark, but it was mine.

Then my doctor asked me a question I didn't see coming: "Do you want an STD test? Often I suggest that to patients getting divorced, especially if they suspect . . ."

Either his voice trailed off—*dot dot dot*—or I don't remember how he finished the sentence. "If they suspect they may need one" or "If they suspect there was infidelity" or "If they suspect their spouse put them at risk." I don't know.

"No, it's okay," I said, mainly because I just didn't want to think about it. I knew divorce had wrecked me emotionally, but the possibility of *physical* risks hadn't even occurred to me. But health is health, and the end of my marriage had been bad for mine. I cried (and cried and cried and cried). I woke up in the middle of the night terrified, my heart racing. I whittled myself down, losing more than twenty pounds. I was thinner than I'd been in high school. I never harmed myself, never planned to, but the darkest moments made me want to disappear. To cut a hole in the air and climb inside. To play a magic trick on my suffering, a sleight of hand.

I didn't disappear.

A NOTE ON THE TITLE

Sometimes I feel like I titled this book *Kittens and Rainbows*, and then I wrote hell.

GHOST STORY

A few months after my husband moved out of the house, I was trying to calm and reassure Rhett, then six years old, at bedtime. He said, "I know, I know. I have a mom who loves me, and I have a dad who loves me. But I don't have a family."

I felt the wind go out of me—felt myself emptying, falling, a balloon drifting down from the ceiling—because he was right. He still had all of his family members, but our family unit, our foursome, was gone.

When people asked how the children were doing, I told them fine. It was mostly true. I told them I was grateful at least that the children didn't lose anyone. They still have their parents and they have each other.

What I didn't say is when I lost my family, I lost someone. The person I'd called my person. In this way, my house is haunted.

THE STAGES

Violet was having friend trouble. Adolescent girls can be cruel, but some of these changes are just a normal part of growing up. Her friend, I told her, was probably trying to figure herself out. She was trying on different friend groups like shirts or jackets to see what felt right to her.

At first my daughter was sad and wanted her friend to come back.

Then she was angry and wanted to know why. How could she *do* that?

Finally she just wanted to be left alone.

Ah yes, I thought. *The stages of divorce.*

A NOTE ON CHARACTER

The last time I was single, I was a teenager. I was living in my parents' house, sleeping in the twin bed I'd had since the first grade, the one with the roll-out trundle. The last time I was single, I had an 11:00 curfew. If I broke it—*when* I broke it—I was grounded.

When my marriage ended, I could picture my life as a time line from a history textbook, eras bracketed for each relationship, one after the other, no space between them:

- my first serious boyfriend (high school)
- my second serious boyfriend (end of high school through college)
- my husband

I was twenty-three when we started dating. He was twenty-two. We were together until our early forties.

If you've always had a significant other, there are two stories you can tell yourself. One is a flattering story: *You're so special, of course you always have someone! You're so cute and funny and smart, you'd never be on the market long.* The other story, the less flattering one, is the one you have to reckon with when you're suddenly single for the first time since you could drive a car: *You're obviously scared to be alone. You're insecure. You'd rather be half of something than whole on your own.*

For the first time in my life, I live alone. Or, not alone exactly, but not with a man. My children are here, my dog is here.

For the first time in my life, there is an opening on the time line, an opening not labeled with a man's name, like the white space between stanzas in a poem.

There are blessings inside every curse.

A NOTE ON PLOT

I picture the narrative arc, the mountain of story we climb from inciting incident to climax. Then we slide down the steep side to resolution. Don't we? Is that promised us?

At any given moment, I wonder: *Is this the rising action? Has the climax already happened or are we not even there yet? When will the crisis end? How will it end? Where is the resolution?*

I crave the answer to *when will it end* even more than the answer to *how.* We can endure anything if we know when it will end.

ON THIS DAY

No, Shutterfly, I don't want to see my life eight years ago today, thanks.

PICTURE OF MY DRESS

@maggiesmithpoet: *Photo essay that won't happen: Divorced woman drives her rumpled c. 2005 wedding dress across the country and takes photos of it in various locations. It's a metaphorical "Weekend at Bernie's" sans stapled-on toupee and sunglasses, because the dead thing is the marriage.*

@mountain_goats: *this would be a song called "Picture of My Dress" imo*

@maggiesmithpoet: *I would play that one on repeat.*

@mountain_goats: *the ideal person to write it would be @M_CCarpenter in my opinion but I'm in the house with 2 kids during winter break for another week so maybe we'll all woodshed it today*

@mountain_goats: *UPDATE: I like to work (screen shot of song file attached)*

@maggiesmithpoet: *I too am in a house with two kids for winter break for another week, so the idea that you can do ANYTHING creative let alone this amazes me. Thank you for doing more with this idea than I could have. I love it.*

Something you should know about me: Music is my constant companion. I listen while writing, cooking, showering, walking my dog, running, folding laundry. When my kids want me to turn it down or turn it off so they can watch TV or do homework, I put on headphones. I listen to music on my good days and my bad days, and music got me through many, many bad days—from finding the postcard to today.

After John Darnielle, the singer-songwriter for The Mountain Goats, and I tweeted back and forth, he sent me the rough track from his home studio. The following March, as news of the pandemic spread and just before lockdown began, John sent photos from Sam Phillips Recording in Memphis. I was sitting at a local bar with friends, and there he was, in front of a music stand in the recording booth. I could see the title on the paper: "Picture of My Dress."

When the band released *Getting Into Knives*, the third track on the record was "Picture of My Dress." The line that gets me every time is this one: "I bless everything there is to bless."

REWINDING THE FILM

There is so much I'd wish to undo. I imagine it, cinematic: I'm putting the postcard back into my husband's work bag, and then his hand is taking it out. Then he's unwriting it, his handwriting disappearing letter by letter from the blank side. And then he's back in the shop where he bought it, putting it back on the carousel of postcards, and he's walking out of the shop backward.

My husband is inserting the cut pages back into his notebook, and then putting it back into his bag, and then I'm putting the notebook back into the bag, because I never saw it, because there was nothing to see, because, look, he's unwriting the pages, his hand moving backward across the page, and where his pen goes, the words disappear.

Over and over again. I see it, like a film. I'm pulling my hands from the bag, walking backward away from where it sat on the dining room chair, sitting back down on the couch again.

But the reversal, the undoing, can't stop there.

I'd have to keep going, to reverse everything that happened before then. Reverse through the business trips, the viral poem, the second book, the second miscarriage, the second law firm, the first miscarriage, the second bout of postpartum depression, the second child, the first law firm, the first bout of postpartum depression, the first child, law school, grad school.

There is so much undoing that needs to happen. By the time my hand slipped into the bag, so much had already happened. Too much, maybe.

There is so much I would wish to undo, if I could go back, go back, go back.

But back to where? Where was it safe?

SOME PEOPLE ASK

"**B**ut you don't regret the marriage, right? Because otherwise you wouldn't have your children?"

People say this all the time. It's not even a question, really—it's a statement. They want confirmation. They want reassurance.

Maybe you're thinking it now, reading this book: *at least she has her children*, or *it was worth it for the children*.

And when people say this, I've paused for a moment. I'm thinking about the cost of answering fully.

—I could say that if not for the marriage, I'd have nothing to tuck in but air. I'd wrap my arms around the air and kiss the air. I'd ask the air how dark it wants its toast, how hot to run the shower water. "How's that?" I'd ask the air, through the closed shower curtain. I could say that sometimes I imagine a Choose Your Own Adventure book. If years ago someone had said, your husband will do X, or your husband will say Y, what would I have done? First of all, and crucially: I wouldn't have believed it. Second of all: If I had believed it, I would've changed paths—turned back to page 22, flipped ahead to page 41. If I'd been convinced, finally, of its truth, its inevitability, I would've chosen a different way. Yes, I know that to undo the marriage, I'd have to undo it all. I would have another marriage. I would be another wife. I would have other children. Yes, I know what I'm saying, but hear me out: I wouldn't miss my children, because they never would have existed! I never would have chosen to put my children—the ones who exist, the ones I love and can't imagine life without—through this—

"I love my children more than anything. I can't imagine life without them." Next question.

What is beautiful alters, has undertow.
                                    —Linda Gregg

BITTERSWEET

keep going back: back to the place where we got engaged, a small cabin in Hocking Hills State Park in southeastern Ohio. For almost fifteen years, we rented it once or twice a year, requesting it by name. We'd pack books, snacks, tea, and red wine. We'd walk in the woods, take baths, read or write in big rocking chairs by the gas fireplace. We ate our meals in the inn's restaurant, housed in a refurbished log cabin. We called it our happy place.

The first time I went alone, I looked across the breakfast table to see the unused place setting: placemat, silverware, coffee mug. I was a one at a two-top. How many times had I sat there, drinking coffee from those handmade pottery mugs, at that very table? How many times had I looked out that very window at those very trees? My tears caught me by surprise. I'd been doing so well. I didn't want him back, so why this sudden grief? I grabbed some cash from my purse for a tip, wedged it under my coffee mug, and left.

It was a full-circle moment, and there would be many of them. Because time is recursive, because we repeat ourselves again and again, because all the things I'd done married I would now do unmarried. Because I was the same and completely different.

The small cabin we always rented was named Bittersweet. Our happy place, Bittersweet. No kidding.

A FRIEND SAYS EVERY
BOOK BEGINS WITH AN
UNANSWERABLE QUESTION

Then what is mine?
how to grieve

MOTHER'S DAY

On my first Mother's Day as a single mother, Rhett brought me my gifts in bed first thing in the morning. He'd wanted to give them to me the night before, but I made him wait for the day itself. I have always been a stickler about traditions.

My bedroom door opened, and I saw his small body silhouetted in the hallway. He was a blur—I hadn't yet grabbed my glasses from the bookshelf beside my bed—but I knew it was him. He crept in and sat down on my bed, handing me some beads, an acorn, and his lucky shark tooth. "Happy Mother's Day!" he said, nestling into me.

When Violet woke up that morning, she came downstairs into the kitchen where I was standing at the counter, making a pour-over. She handed me a piece of paper: an "About My Mom" Q&A her teacher had given out to the whole class for Mother's Day. *What has your mom taught you?* one question read. *To be optimistic*, Violet had written.

Optimistic?! To say I was surprised would be an understatement. It had been a brutal eleven months for me. For all of us. That my daughter had witnessed me struggling for months and saw hope? There was no better gift.

That night we laughed so hard at dinner that we all fell out of our chairs. Literally. Rhett said, "You're the best mom. There's nobody more fun than you." Dinner at our house is informal, even raucous at times. There are spontaneous comedy bits, impressions, dance moves. We joke, "I'm sure all of the other families in all the other houses are doing the same thing at this moment," and we laugh.

After dinner, we snuggled up on the couch together. Rhett was reading on one side of the sectional, but Violet made a nest for me with her legs, and I curled up in it with my head resting on her hip while she began *To Kill a Mockingbird* again (reading it for the second time). Our dog tucked herself into the nest I made for her, with her nose in the backs of my knees. When I was a kid, my dad used to do just this: sit on the couch and make a nest with his legs for me, or at least *nest* is what I called it when he made room for me behind his knees.

Curled up together on the couch, Brandi Carlisle playing on the stereo, I had to stay very still so no one would know I was weepy from the deeply-at-home-and-at-peace feeling.

ABOUT THE BODY

For years I'd joked that my body was basically a plant stand for my head. I lived from the neck up, but obviously I knew I needed the rest of it to get me around, to keep me going. I fed and watered myself now and then.

The body is full of surprises, some wonderful, some terrible. Like, if all the blood vessels in your body were laid end to end, they would reach about sixty thousand miles. The veins of the average child could wind around the Earth twice; an adult, three times. Or, the average human dream lasts only two to three seconds. Your thigh bone, the femur, is stronger than concrete. And hollow.

The body is full of surprises, and it has the power to surprise us again and again. When my marriage ended, it got loud in my head, as loud and crowded as an obnoxious party where no one is having a good time. I wanted out of there. I couldn't leave—there are no Irish exits from one's own head—but maybe I could make staying more livable. Maybe I could quiet my mind by allowing my body to be loud, present, in the foreground for once.

I tried yoga, meditation, long walks. I went dancing late at night with my friend Dawn—to live in my body instead of my head, I said. We'd sweat and laugh for hours, then stumble outside onto High Street at 2:00 in the morning, wrung out and happy.

My friend Sergei suggested running might be a good way for me to manage stress. He recommended the app Couch to 5K, so I downloaded it, with no intention of running a 5K, but I did start running. At first I ran for two minutes, then walked for two minutes, then ran again. A voice in the app would tell me what to do: "Slow down and walk," or "Now run." Each day the intervals shifted slightly: run for three, walk for two; run for five, walk for one.

When the woman's voice told me to run, I groaned, loud enough that anyone around could hear me. Sometimes I'd talk back to that robotic sadist: *Give me a fucking break.* Or, just an emphatic and exhausted *Fuuuuuuuck.*

When she told me to stop running and walk, I would actually say *Thank you*. You catch more flies with honey, they say. Maybe some gratitude would change the algorithm and she'd go easier on me next time?

At the end of one run, I stopped, bent over, my hands on my thighs, and laughed. Really belly-laughed, just standing on the sidewalk in front of my house. I didn't know my body could do that. There is joy in surprising oneself.

THE FIRSTS

Violet lost her last baby tooth at her father's house, a molar, which means I have all of her tiny, shell-sharp teeth in an earring box in my jewelry drawer, tucked in the way back, except one. And her father has a single molar of hers somewhere.

When he moved out of our house, he took essentials. He left behind the bird's nest we found in the Christmas tree we had when our daughter was a newborn. He left behind family photos and the kids' refrigerator drawings. There were things he left behind that I would've run into a burning house to retrieve. I'm attached to my children's things, to the stuff of their childhood. Does this mean I'm motherly or simply nostalgic? Rhett now sleeps with the doll I had as a baby—Pink Baby. He loves the way her plastic face feels smooth and cool, separate from the softness of her stuffed body. I loved that, too, when I was a girl.

My bedroom dresser is covered with framed photos—my children mainly, but also my late grandmother, my dog, and one of me at age seven in my Brownie uniform. The frame is wood and bordered with popsicle sticks. My smile is part baby teeth, part adult.

I'm notoriously squeamish about loose teeth. Once, when the dentist pulled a very wiggly baby tooth for Violet, I was so lightheaded I half jokingly asked for a Sprite. I've happily relied on Mrs. Tyson, the school nurse, to snap on her gloves and yank out the ones that were so loose, my daughter couldn't eat her lunch.

When Rhett's first baby tooth was really loose, I was about to leave for a ten-day trip to LA, teaching for an MFA summer residency. I worried that my six-year-old might lose his first tooth while I was gone. I worried that my son's first tooth fairy visit would be at a house my ex-husband had rented. I worried that I'd miss the first.

So I iced the tooth. I wiggled it around, then tried to pull it. Started sweating a little. I wiggled it again. Iced again. Tried again. I realize how completely bizarre this sounds now, but at the time . . .

Dot dot dot.

My son's tooth was still in his mouth when his father picked him up. It wasn't ready to come out. It wanted to stay where it was.

ON SECOND THOUGHT

How can I tell *mine* if I can't find it? If I'm still out with lanterns. If the questions are burning, burning, burning—and the omniscient narrator, the one with all the answers, is nowhere to be found.

What I'm living and experiencing is my life, but what about the rest? If I know so little about the life I've called my own, if there are blank spaces I can't fill in, can I still call it my life? Can I still claim it as mine?

GHOST STORY

The summer after my husband moved out, I discovered an Australian show called *Glitch*. In the first episode, several people claw their way from their graves—naked, muddy, disoriented. They have no idea what has happened, no idea that they died five or twenty or even a hundred years earlier. The six of them are inexplicably alive again, the age they were when they died. For them, no time has passed.

Their bodies have been restored. A woman who'd died of breast cancer unbuttons her shirt before a mirror and sees her breasts—the ones a surgeon had removed. They're perfect. No scars.

Spoiler alert: Her husband is the police officer called to the cemetery.

Spoiler alert: After the woman died, he married her best friend.

Spoiler alert: The new wife—the old best friend—is nine months pregnant.

The woman, her breasts buttoned up inside her shirt, is a witness to the afterlife. She returns to the life that continued without her. In one scene she's in the baby's nursery in the house that was her house. Who wouldn't touch the mobile above the crib? It spins. She haunts. No scars? I cried when I watched the show as if for her.

How I picture it: A scar tells a story, a very short story about pain, injury, healing—what so much great literature is about. A scar is concise communication.

The white hyphen on my wrist from the clasp of my watch tells a story. I don't have that watch anymore, or the apartment I lived in then, or the person I lived with, but the punctuation—the symbol for connection, yoking one word to another, making a new whole—is still here.

The little white line under my son's chin, an em dash, tells a story. He slipped and fell in the bathtub, only three years old, and as I lifted him from the water I saw his bone, the skin pulled away like pictures in books of seals, whales, the layer of fat under the slick skin. I rocked and sang him to sleep, naked, swaddled in a damp bath towel, one corner held against his chin to stop the bleeding, while we waited for his father to come home from an evening event and drive us to the hospital.

The long pink line where my daughter left my body, then my son, tells a story. A door opened, then shut, then opened and shut again. But I have stood ajar since the moment I became a mother.

SURE YOU ARE

In June, a few months into the separation but before the divorce was final, I flew to Los Angeles to teach a graduate-level poetry workshop. It was the university's summer MFA residency, and they brought in visiting faculty across genres from all over the country. I felt lucky to be invited and very glad to get to spend time with some other poet friends who I typically only saw at the AWP conference once a year.

My itinerary was packed: daily workshops, craft lectures, readings, student conferences, panel discussions. I walked a couple of miles back and forth between my hotel to the academic complex two or three times a day, listening to music: Nada Surf, Superchunk, The New Pornographers, Yo La Tengo. I remember the strange, twisted trees, unlike Ohio trees, full of barking crows.

I was weaning myself off Lexapro and had started quartering the pills I'd previously been cutting in half. First I'd tried to stop cold turkey, but then there were the "brain zaps," like an electrical storm inside my skull. I decided to wean myself off instead, taking half of my prescribed dose each day. With even the tiniest amount inside me, the lightning stopped. There were no black footprints where I stood.

The pills were tiny to begin with, and quartering them on the bathroom counter in my hotel room was tricky work. When you use a dull pill-splitter to cut a tiny white tablet into four crumbs, you end up with more dust than pill. The bitter taste in my mouth seemed fitting. I could almost laugh.

"The best time to wean yourself off meds for anxiety and depression is in the middle of a bitter, expensive divorce," I joked to my friend Victoria, who directed the MFA program. Yes, I laughed, as I always do. Under all comedy is tragedy. Under the boat, the water that holds us is dark and full of things we can't see.

I was going off the medication in part because I thought I could manage without it, and in part because I would lose my health insurance the day the divorce decree was signed by the judge. I didn't know if I'd be able to afford my prescription. Better to be safe than sorry and teach my body not to need it. When I flew back to Ohio from California, I'd be done.

While I was teaching in LA, Violet and Rhett would stay with my parents for half of the time and with their father for the other half. Five days in one place, five days in the other. I thought they were home with him—it was Father's Day weekend—but when I finally got ahold of the kids that afternoon, they were out of state with "Dad's friend [The Addressee]."

I'd describe what happened next in my hotel room as an anxiety attack. I was in California during the time people call "June gloom," a period of typically overcast skies, and my children were with their father and The Addressee on the other side of the country. I remember thinking he'd made his mess their mess, too. Now they were in it. He took them to it, then had the nerve to claim they chose the location for the road trip. All coincidence.

I called my mother. I spoke with my dear friends Ann and Kelly on the phone, pacing back and forth between the bed and the window in my hotel room. *Spoke* isn't quite the right word. How about: *fumed, freaked out, cried*. Eventually, later that evening, I spoke with my husband, even though we hadn't spoken on the phone since well before the separation. I had left a faculty reading to take his call and was huddled in a classroom, sitting at a long seminar table, trying to keep my voice down. It came down to this: What business did I have criticizing his parenting when I was off in LA?

"I'm *working*!" I said.

His response? "Sure you are."

IT WASN'T ALL BAD

Reader, I want you to know that trip to LA was beautiful in plenty of ways. It was more than *sure you are*. It was more than quartered pills on the bathroom counter, more than pacing the hotel room until I could've burned a path of black footprints into the carpet. There were no footprints.

What there was, that June in California, was friendship, community, a sense of purpose, and the Pacific.

I had breakfast with Victoria at the diner from *The Big Lebowski*, the one where the nihilists, including Flea and Aimee Mann, order lingonberry pancakes. Yes, I ordered pancakes, and we talked about everything that had gone wrong—and everything that was still going right. Just *being there* was something that was going right. Each morning I taught a poetry workshop, and I felt free—free to be myself and do my work without asking for permission or forgiveness.

The last weekend I was in Los Angeles, an old college friend picked me up at my hotel and took me to Venice Beach. I'd never seen the Pacific Ocean up close. Jeremy and I walked on the pier, then stopped at a little place for Mexican food and giant margaritas. I got beautifully drunk—not sick, not tired, just happy—and we walked to the water, took off our shoes, and waded in calf-deep. I felt quieted, calmed, like when you whisper to a spooked horse to settle it: *whoa now, easy now*. I was remembering how to be. Not a mother, not a teacher, not even a writer. Just me.

A NOTE ON BETRAYAL

Betrayal is neat because it is absolving. *I couldn't save my marriage*, I thought, *because I didn't have the whole truth.* There were variables I didn't understand. Still, I tried. I thought, if we both did the work, we could make it. I believed that.

So when he asked me to stop traveling for work, to stay home, I agreed. I agreed to make my life smaller, my writing less important, because I thought that would make him happy.

But he was still unkind, still distant. Why? I asked. Because he didn't think I would stick to it. He thought I'd start traveling again eventually, that the writing wouldn't stay small. That I wouldn't be satisfied or content if I folded it up and set it aside.

Here's the thing: He was right. It wouldn't have lasted. But who tries to save their marriage by making their partner choose between being who they are, doing what they do, and being married? I would have chosen being married, and I would have been miserable. And then it would have ended anyway.

AIR QUOTES

After I returned from California, in a meeting in my lawyer's office—my lawyer and I on one side of the conference table, my husband and his on the other—my husband's lawyer used air quotes when she talked about my work.

When you were "working," she said.

Writing is work that can hold up its head with all the other kinds of useful work out there in the world, and it is genuinely work.

—Rebecca Solnit

THE PLAY

There is no set for The Attorney's office. No conference room behind double glass doors, no table, no chairs.

The cast is asymmetrical, off-kilter: three lawyers, one poet. The cast is three people who've had meetings like this before, one person who hasn't. The cast is three apples and an orange.

The Finder is holding a small, jagged piece of rose quartz in her right hand under the table. She rubs it to stay calm and centered. We don't see the backstory of that piece of rose quartz. Marie, a writer The Finder met during the writing residency in Virginia—the residency The Finder left at two in the morning, spiraling down a mountain road in the rain—mailed her the rose quartz for its healing properties when The Finder announced her divorce. Also in the care package: a tincture and an illustrated postcard of Audre Lorde that reads "I am who I am, doing what I came to do."

There is no flashback scene of The Finder meeting Marie, no scene of Marie making the tincture or mailing the package. There's no scene of The Finder driving to The Attorney's office, listening to Cat Power's "Woman" on repeat, loud. No scene of her singing along: "I'm a woman of my word, now haven't you heard / My word's the only thing I've ever needed." There's no scene in which The Finder quiets her mind before the meeting, giving herself three rules to follow, no matter what: 1. Do not cry, 2. Do not lose your temper, 3. Communicate your points. There's no scene in which she does not cry, does not yell, and—rubbing the rose quartz under the table to stay focused—communicates her points. The Finder's laptop is open in front of her on the conference room table. She has not been in a room with The Husband in months, but she's prepared.

There is no scene in the play in which The Finder leaves the meeting and meets her friend Ann for a midday drink. Two oranges, no apples in sight. There is no scene to show this symmetry because there is no play, only life. In the life, The Finder reminds herself of two things:

> *I am who I am, doing what I came to do.*
> *My word's the only thing I've ever needed.*

A FRIEND SAYS EVERY BOOK BEGINS WITH AN UNANSWERABLE QUESTION

Then what is mine?
how to remain myself

EMPIRE BUILDER

That August I was in a small sleeping car, a roomette, with my friend Wendy. This was supposed to be my post-divorce, *Thelma and Louise* meets *White Christmas* adventure. I had romanticized the idea of train travel for a hundred reasons, most of them film related. Danny Kaye, Bing Crosby, Rosemary Clooney, and Vera-Ellen sitting in the booth in the dining car, singing "Snow," draping the white napkin, making a mountain and tiny pines? That tops the list.

But it wasn't post-divorce at all. Litigation had dragged on and on. We can endure anything if we know when it will end, but I had no idea when it would end. (Reader, when I first wrote these sentences, it still hadn't ended.)

Wendy and I flew from Columbus to Chicago, took a car to the train station, then boarded a train that runs from Chicago to Seattle—the Empire Builder, as in the American Empire, westward expansion, railroad wealth. As in *where all of this is once was nothing.*

Wendy and I had watched YouTube videos of the roomette layout before we booked the trip, unsure of how much space we'd have (or need). What we had was a tiny room with two seats facing each other across a small table. Each night the porter, Jay, came to prepare our beds. He tucked the table away and folded the two seats down to form the lower bunk. He pulled the narrow top bunk bed down from the ceiling, and made up both beds with fresh sheets. Each morning he came to strip them and fold them away.

I was the one riding backward in this roomette. The train pushed me back through Illinois, Wisconsin, Minnesota, North Dakota, Montana, and Idaho, to Washington. As we rolled by farms, silos, small towns, depots, salvage yards, quarries, foundries, tanneries, I looked toward what was behind us, what we were leaving. Sometimes a metaphor occurs to me in the moment. This one came to me as I wrote it just now. I wasn't traveling *into* the landscape but being ripped from it. Or I was being propelled backward into it, invisible hands on my chest pushing me back, back, back.

Almost twenty years before, Wendy and I met because our husbands worked together. When we took the trip, my husband was living across town, and the divorce was nearly final. Her husband had taken a temporary Peace Corps position overseas. We were both on our own that summer, though the circumstances were different.

I wrote in my notebook; she painted with a tiny watercolor set in her sketchbook. We walked down to the dining car for meals, where we always shared our table with strangers, mostly retired couples who'd done this before. Most of the time I didn't know where we were. I didn't know what state I was in. The metaphor occurred to me in the moment: *Where am I? What does it matter, really? I'm in the in-between—not where I was, not where I'm going.* In my earbuds, Gillian Welch sang, "Everything Is Free," and I couldn't decide if I believed that. So much of life felt expensive then: Everything had a cost, and I don't mean money.

One morning the year before, my husband had woken up, and as we lay in bed he tried to explain what was wrong. It was like he woke up and this was his life, and he didn't know how any of it had happened.

In the months leading up to the train trip, I had thought a lot about what people call "a midlife crisis." What is the crisis, exactly: traveling through your life on a track, on the force of your own momentum, at the mercy of your own momentum, the landscape only a blur? And what is the remedy? To get off the train, to swear off trains entirely, to say, "What train?"

The landscape rolled by like a filmstrip: the dark movie of Minnesota followed by North Dakota, which I slept through much of. I woke knowing I'd had strange dreams, but I couldn't remember what they were. In sleep, the body is still, but the mind is moving. The mind still moves.

Sometimes the film was set in a swamp with trees and moss, like the cover of a book I had as a child. It was a mystery. Sometimes the film went tree, tree, tree, tree, tree, the moon playing the high notes at the top of the register. Sometimes it went depot, farms, silos, small towns. Or salvage yard, foundry, tannery, quarry, lake. Once, there was a deer under a freight train on the adjacent tracks. Ducks swimming in a pond. Miles of wheat. Fields blond and shorn, the sky above them washed out, barely blue, diluted. Even in daylight the half moon was visible, a little sticker half peeled off.

At the Rugby, North Dakota, depot, a sign: The Geographical Center of North America. I jotted it down in my notebook, thinking about what it means to be at the center, thinking about being the center that holds as one's surroundings fly apart, fly away. Like the eye of a storm. Like the Gravitron, that ride, a centrifuge.

I wasn't distorted across state lines, from EST to MST to PST. I was still me, watching the film playing in the windows, balanced on that thin boundary between thinking and feeling. I was crossing through landscapes, through time zones, across boundaries, and I was me, regardless.

GEN X FOREVER & EVER, AMEN

When my marriage ended, I did the thing we all do after a breakup: I tortured myself by listening to sad-ass songs on repeat, like pressing a bruise. Once that masochistic phase came to its natural conclusion—once I stopped needing the Sufjan Stevens and Bon Iver and Low, so much Low—I found myself gravitating toward early '90s indie rock: Pavement, Heatmiser, Liz Phair, The Breeders, Pixies, Dinosaur Jr. It didn't occur to me until months later that these were all bands I loved in high school and college, before I met my husband, as if I were trying to remind myself of who I was before—the woman who predated not only the divorce but also the marriage. I predated this shit, the music reminded me, and I would outlast it.

THE VISION PART OF THE BOARD

In the middle of the divorce, a friend invited me to a vision board workshop. I didn't attend because my vision board would've looked a lot like Mark Rothko's *Untitled (Black on Gray)*. In Rothko's painting, the bottom half of the canvas is gray and the top half is black, as if it's risen to the rim of some murky glass. The black floats on the gray. Or it's city concrete, a horizon line, the sky matte black.

My vision of the future was dark and abstract. I woke up each morning and wrote a note-to-self, a little pep talk—"keep moving"—not because I thought other people needed them, but because I needed them.

But look at the painting again: the black floats. There is buoyancy implied. This is the vision part of the board.

QUARTER MISSING

When my—*our*—children first had overnight visits at their father's rental house, I thought of myself as the quarter missing. When the three of them were together, they were three-quarters of the family we once were. We were asymmetrical and off-kilter. Incomplete.

Early on, sometimes I woke in the night and couldn't remember if Violet and Rhett were in the house or not. I couldn't remember if they were sleeping in their beds. I'd retrace the trail of narrative breadcrumbs: bedtime, toothbrushing, books, songs, tuck-in conversations. I'd think of what day it was. The kids split time between our houses then, so Mondays and Tuesdays were always mine.

Some mornings I'd do the same. Waking, still groggy, it took me a minute to remember if they were with me or with their father. Was my house three-quarters empty or three-quarters full?

"I have the kids today," I said, when they were at my house. As in: They're mine today. As in: Today I have children.

The poems are mine. I have sole custody. All of them, every day.

SELF-PORTRAIT

Violet came home from school one day and dropped her backpack near the stairs.

"How was your day, sis? What was the best part?" I asked.

"In art we had to do self-portraits," she said. "Mrs. Reiser gave us mirrors, and we had to draw ourselves from the shoulders up."

She unzipped her backpack and pulled out the portrait, handing it to me.

"Oh, Vi, this is beautiful." The penciled hair was a veil, one piece of lace.

"I couldn't make it look like me," she said. "I couldn't get the eyes right."

"Well, we can't see ourselves any way but backward," I told her. "We don't see ourselves the way other people see us." I knew how hard she'd tried, how hard she always tries. I pictured her biting her lip, brushing bits of eraser from the paper, looking again and again at the reversal of her face, trying to get it right.

THE PROFILE

I remember exactly where I was—sitting on the edge of my bed—when a friend texted: *OMG I just found [my husband's name] on [dating app].*

I saw—*dot dot dot*—that she was typing more. *I can send you screenshots if you want to see them. Or not if you don't want to! I don't want to hurt you.*

No, it doesn't hurt, I texted back. *Please send.*

She sent me screenshots. Selfies. A written profile. It is surreal to say the least, seeing the online dating profile of a person you are still legally married to, someone who is still technically your husband. Someone you lived with for eighteen years. It's even more than surreal—an absolute mindfuck, to be clear—to realize you probably wouldn't match with your own spouse, or at least not with this version of him. *On the bright side,* I thought, *maybe the relationship with The Addressee ended, and he's looking for someone local. Maybe we can move on from that part of the story.*

I wonder what I would put in my own dating profile. Poet, writer, single mother of two, Gen Xer, lifelong Ohioan, city mouse, vegetarian. Loves books, live music, travel, dogs not cats, black coffee and black tattoos, dark beer and dark chocolate. Self-employed. Author of several books. Liberal, pro-choice, agnostic, monogamous. Aquarius. Gregarious introvert. Funny as hell. Occasionally melancholic. Good cook. Bad sleeper. Woman who, let's be real, probably won't trust you. Woman who will try.

GHOST STORY

When their father first moved out of the house, the children would spend two days with me, then two days with him; five days with me, then five days with him. I worked from home, so I would pick up the children from school every day, even on his days, and he would pick them up from my house on his way home. If he was working late, I'd feed the kids dinner.

He would park his car in my driveway and walk up in his suit. He grew a beard, so he looked like a doppelganger of himself. Or like a dream, when someone looks almost like the person you know but something is off: They're suddenly left-handed. Or their laugh sounds recorded and played backward. I kept waiting to wake up, but I was awake.

I knew the time would come when I'd witness the afterlife. The new house, certainly, with some of our old things inside. The new wife, likely— someone else who would tuck my children in.

This is a story of becoming embodied, impossible to walk straight through.

When their father came to collect them, I kissed my son and daughter and sent them toward the waiting car. I closed the door and locked it. If I had chains to rattle, I would have rattled my chains.

How I picture it: The divorce is like the Big Bang—not a single event with an aftermath, but something set in motion—a spillage, an overflowing, an expansion. The universe is still expanding, but it happens so slowly we don't feel it or see it. The universe slipped the gate and kept running. It keeps running.

The Big Bang is not something in the past, but something that continues, relentlessly, via litigation, via renegotiating, via emails and texts, via calls from lawyers and parenting coordinators.

The divorce is a continuation of the marriage. Something set in motion years ago that continues.

SIGNING THE PAPERS

After over a year of litigation, it took me just a few minutes to sign the divorce papers in my lawyer's office. When I walked in the door, I was married. *Mrs.* When I walked outside, I was divorced. *Ms.* That was *it*?

Afterward, because I was in the neighborhood, I drove to Pistacia Vera, my favorite bakery. Parking in German Village is notoriously difficult, so the closest spot I could find was right in front of my old house, the brick Victorian with gingerbread trim where we'd lived when Violet was born.

Sitting at a café table on the bakery's patio, I cried a little behind my sunglasses, drinking my coffee, picking at a flaky chocolate croissant. I wasn't sad because I wanted to be married to him, I just couldn't believe that all of it added up to . . . *this*? All of those years—gone. *Poof.*

I remember thinking, *What now? What do I have now? What do I have to hold on to?*

When I looked down, I saw the pen in my hand.

I am not alone. Whatever else there was or is, writing is with me.

—Lidia Yuknavitch

THE POEM

I have poems that have accrued over eight, nine, ten years. Sometimes it feels like each poem I write is a draft of The Poem I'm trying to write—that singular, golden, impossibly definitive poem. The one poem I'm trying to live. Or the one life I'm trying to write. The *mine*.

I've been testing out so many metaphors in this book, trying to find the perfect imagistic shorthand for this heartpunch of an experience—the boat, the water, the nesting dolls, the ghosts, the scars—but this story isn't reducible to one. There isn't a singular, golden, impossibly definitive metaphor that encapsulates everything. No, it's all of them. I'm handing you a stack of Polaroids to shuffle in your hands, so some of the work is yours.

LEMONADE

Every day through my divorce, I posted a note-to-self on social media, each one ending with the same words: *Keep moving.* When I announced that these quotes would be published as a book, a friend commented on my post: "You took those lemons and made lemonade, and then you added MF vodka to it."

I think I responded with a laugh-cry emoji. I understood what she meant: The worst had happened, and somehow I'd made something good—something beautiful—from it. But then I thought about the cost of that lemonade. I thought about my friend Kelly, who, after publishing a memoir about her abusive marriage, endured comments like "at least you got a book out of it." *At least you got a book out of it?!* As if she should be thankful in some way for her suffering, because it gave her "material"?

I'm trying to tell you the truth, so let me be clear: I didn't want this lemonade. My kids didn't want this lemonade. This lemonade was not worth the lemons. And yet, the lemons were mine. I had to make something from them, so I did. I wrote.

I'll drink to that.

THE PLAY

How many acts are in this imagined play? Three sounds neat, doesn't it? Marriage, divorce, and then . . . ? Where there had been a future, or at least the promise of one, there was now an ellipsis. *Dot dot dot.*

Three acts sounds neat, but life isn't neat. The play continues, and there is no indication of when it might end. In a new scene, a scene leafed in between others at the last minute, The Finder (formerly known as The Wife) has a brief monologue about flowers. She's arranging some of her favorites—hydrangeas, tulips, ranunculus, spider mums, snapdragons—in a vase. She's softly spotlit, talking to herself in an empty room.

The thing is, flowers die when you pick them. As soon as you cut them and put them in a vase, the clock's on. You're displaying them as something beautiful, and the whole time they're decomposing. Sometimes I think our marriage was like that. As soon as it began, it was beginning to end.

PHOTO ESSAY THAT WON'T HAPPEN

I still think about taking my wedding dress on a road trip. I still think about taking pictures of it—the first wedding dress I tried on, bought on sale at a strip mall bridal store for $250—in various sentimental locations, leaving a scrap of white satin behind, the way you might scatter ashes. Where would I leave a piece of a dead marriage?

The Perkins restaurant outside Gettysburg, Pennsylvania, where we ate pancakes for dinner and tried to remember the name of the ice-cream shop we'd seen on the business route into town: The Distelfink. One of us called it *Whifflebinks* and we laughed until we cried. The servers side-eying us as they passed probably thought we were high.

The Red Key Tavern in Indianapolis, a dive bar where you could order a beer and a candy bar, and where Kurt Vonnegut was never a regular, though for years I believed that lore.

Golden Gate Park, San Francisco, though the memory of that place is all but gone now, so I have to rely on my own poetry to reconstruct the imagery—magnolia trees, the flowers blown down.

The barn-roofed house in Delaware, Ohio, where he lived in college. I could tuck a little piece under the twin bed in the tiny room where I undressed and hung my clothes over the back of his wooden desk chair, where we slept by the window, the landlord's son waking us by mowing the lawn too early on Saturdays, filling the room with the scent of cut grass.

Sedona, Arizona, where we honeymooned, where I remember seeing a white smudge of Milky Way I wanted to wipe away. It made a mess of the sky.

The Grand Canyon, or maybe Oak Creek Canyon, which we had to drive along to get there from Sedona. I had an anxiety attack. I can say "I had an anxiety attack on my honeymoon" and laugh now about how that was prescient. I was afraid of heights and in the passenger side, on the cliff's edge, I felt completely out of control. No, I *was* completely out of control. I wasn't driving. I could float a white scrap down to the water winding below.

Every room of this house in Ohio, every surface our hands have touched, every glass or fork or spoon that's known our mouths.

Or a state I've never visited, in the park I've never seen, beneath the pine trees I know are there because a pinecone made its way to my house.

Everywhere I go from now on, I could cut a strip of satin from the dress until there is no dress, as now there is no bride to wear it.

I bless everything there is to bless.

JOKE

One afternoon Rhett came home from school with a joke book. He opened it up and read to me from one of the pages: "What is bigger than an elephant but weighs nothing?"

I answered instantly: "An elephant's shadow."

He looked at me, eyes narrowed, suspicious. "Did you look? How did you know that?"

—I know because I've been dragging my old, married name around for more than a year—on my social security card, on my bank accounts, on my driver's license, on my tax return, on my credit card, on my checks, on my mail. I know because my marriage is gone—weighs nothing—but its shadow weighs a ton—

"Just a good guess, buddy."

How I picture it: A scar is a story about pain, injury, healing. Years, too, are scars we wear. I remember their stories.

The year everything changed. Kindergarten, fourth grade. The year of the pinecone, the postcard, the notebook. The year of waking in the night, sweating, heart racing. The year of being the only adult in the house, one baseball bat by the front door and another one under the bed.

Or the year the divorce was finalized. First grade, fifth grade. Two houses, two beds, two Christmases, two birthdays. The year of where are your rain boots, they must be at Dad's house. The year of who signed the permission slip? The year of learning to mow the lawn. The year of fixing the lawn mower, unclogging the toilets. The year I was tattooed with lemons. The year of sleeping with the dog instead of a husband. (The dog snores more quietly. The dog takes up less space.) The year of tweeting a note-to-self every day to keep myself moving. The year I kept moving. The year of sitting up at night, forgetting whether the kids were asleep in their beds or not. The year of waking in the morning and having to remember whether they were with me. The year I feared I would lose the house, and the year I did not lose the house. The year I wanted to cut a hole in the air and climb inside, and the year I didn't want that at all. The year I decided not to disappear. The year I decided not to be small. The year I lived.

THE SECOND CHRISTMAS

It was my second Christmas since my marriage ended but my first Christmas morning without my kids—the first time they weren't here overnight on Christmas Eve, the first year I didn't get to see them run down the stairs to see their filled stockings and presents from Santa under the tree.

I woke up that morning around 7:00 as usual. Our shared parenting agreement stipulated that the children would be dropped off at my house at noon. Five hours. I could do this. Downstairs I turned on the Christmas lights, let the dog out and filled her bowl with food, then went back upstairs to put on my winter running clothes. I did my best to outrun my sadness, my usual playlist cycling through Prince, Metric, Talking Heads, Neko Case, The Clash. I took my favorite route around my neighborhood, passing houses lit with Christmas or Hannukah lights, and the one plastic nativity with Joseph tipped over in the grass, Mary and the baby Jesus still upright, managing on their own. (*Tale as old as time*, I thought to myself.)

Back at home, flushed and sweaty, I put the kettle on for coffee before showering. From the kitchen I heard the doorbell. When I opened the front door, embarrassed at how disheveled I looked—bedhead, sweat, running tights—I saw Taylor, my neighbor a block over. She was standing on the porch holding her youngest daughter, a toddler with bright red curls. She held out a paper plate to me, covered in foil.

"I saw you run by the house, and I remembered that you were alone this morning. I remember that first holiday alone without my son." I heard the emotion in her voice. Tears welled up in her eyes. "So I brought you some cake."

I took the plate and thanked her, and tried to keep myself from crying until after I closed the door behind me. Then I stood at my kitchen counter, making a very strong pour-over, eating orange cake with my hands. I was still in my sweaty running clothes, my hair a mess. I heard another knock at the door.

When I opened it, there was my next-door neighbor, Barb, holding out a box of pastries from a local Greek bakery. "I know this year is a tough one. I thought you could use these."

Like the previous Christmas, so much sweetness. I was not alone.

A NOTE ON MOTIFS

I remember now: In the short play about the cheating spouse, the tip-off is the friend's cologne. He smells, recognizes, knows.

As my children would certainly tell you, I have a *thing* for perfume. Each day I choose a favorite from my sizeable collection—Maison Margiela By the Fireplace, Le Labo Rose 31, Henry Rose Queens & Monsters, Tokyo-Milk Dark Arsenic, Issey Miyaki Butterfly, Memo Paris French Leather. I leave a trace of myself, ghostlike, on my clothes, my sheets, my pillows. At bedtime, Rhett snuggles in close to me and buries his face in my chest—for "the mommy smell," he says. He breathes me in. Recognizes me. Knows.

A NOTE ON SETTING

Setting isn't just place, but time. When the pandemic began, the world seemed to shut like a door. The grocery store shelves were empty of bread, the streets were empty of cars. The news arrived each day with stories of overcrowded ERs, ventilator shortages, quarantine protocols.

The news each day was death.

Suddenly the ways my children's father and I hurt each other seemed so small.

All the marquees said We'll Be Back.

QUARANTINE SKATE CLUB

My first and best pandemic purchase was a pair of aqua roller skates with bright-pink wheels and laces, and in the first weeks of Ohio's shelter-in-place order, my friend Wendy and I met for what we called "Quarantine Skate Club."

Picture it: a couple of middle-aged women roller-skating at a safe distance from one another in a driveway, listening to disco, laughing too hard despite quizzical looks from the neighbors. It saved me some days.

Wendy was in charge of the playlist. She'd bring out her Bluetooth speaker, set it up on a camp chair, and we'd skate up and down her long driveway and into the alley behind her house. I'd text her if the weather was decent: *Skate later?* She'd text back: *I'll be out there in 15*. And because no one was going anywhere, I was imminently available. My house is right across the street, after all. If it was after 3:00 I'd take a beer with me, or she'd mix up cocktails for us. I once scheduled an interview with the *Washington Post* around my QSC schedule. I kept eyeing my phone, pulling it out of the front pocket of my overalls, to make sure I wasn't late getting home for the call.

Quarantine was a learning experience. Among its lessons: I can roller-skate backward with a margarita in one hand.

Once while turning around in the alley, I saw a man come out of his house into his backyard, wearing a button-down shirt and tie on top, plaid pajama pants and slippers on the bottom. I was wearing a sleeveless dress, rainbow-striped tube socks, and turquoise and pink roller skates. We made eye contact across the alley and both started laughing. We were zooming in our own ways.

I'd been insisting on joy, clawing my way back to it, since the divorce. I had plenty of practice in making the best of things. I started skating when the kids were at their dad's, but once they heard about it, they wanted to come sometimes, too. Violet was learning on roller skates, and Rhett had a skateboard.

I'd text Wendy: *Can we use your driveway?* Rhett would carry his skateboard over, and I'd bring my skates and my phone for music, and on those days, he got to DJ. We could usually agree on Superchunk. We'd roll by each other and high-five, or hold hands with him rolling on his board and me rolling on my skates. We laughed so hard, I think we probably brought some joy to the people who saw us as they drove or walked by: a mother and son making the best of it.

Once he looked at me and said, "This is who we are now."

Here's a little taste of our QSC playlist. Don't say I never gave you anything.

"Got to Be Real," Cheryl Lynn
"I Feel for You," Chaka Khan
"She's a Bad Mama Jama," Carl Carlton
"Ring My Bell," Anita Ward
"More Bounce to the Ounce," Zapp
"Le Freak," CHIC
"Best of My Love," The Emotions
"You Dropped a Bomb on Me," The Gap Band
"Forget Me Nots," Patrice Rushen
"I'm Coming Out," Diana Ross
"Let's Groove," Earth, Wind & Fire
"Xanadu," Olivia Newton-John
"Night Fever," Bee Gees
"Love Rollercoaster," Ohio Players
"Get Down on It," Kool & The Gang

EMAIL, SUBJECT LINE: UPDATE

He's moving to a new rental house in our neighborhood, and he's engaged to The Addressee. She and her kids will split their time between here and there. They'll be blending their families in the new house.

How I picture it: The distance I must keep between us and anyone else is the size of my children's father. To stay six feet away from anyone, I carry like a mental yardstick the image of him lying flat on his back, his head at my feet. He isn't sleeping. No, he looks up at me, upside down. This is the closest we've been in years, but only in my imagination. Wherever I go, his apparition precedes me.

Even the neighborhood trees are distanced. I can't not notice them now, the intervals at which they were planted: at least six feet between them and between the nests squirrels built in their uppermost branches.

The pear trees, just beginning to blossom, hold high their fistfuls of dry leaves.

IT'S STILL THERE

In the beginning of the pandemic, someone jokingly tweeted, "What did you do to cause this?" My reply, one of many: "I said out loud that I was happy." And I was.

I began the year as a newly divorced single mom; I'd been on my own for over a year, but I wasn't alone, not really. I was focusing on myself and my children, cultivating my friendships, traveling, writing. I was making a new life for myself, and I was surprised by how at home I felt in it.

For most of my life, I'd been a planner—driven and organized in my work; wedded to a schedule as a parent. But both the divorce and the pandemic meant a loss of control. So many of the things I had planned for were no longer possible, and I had to let go. I loosened my white-knuckled grip on my life and instead of feeling panicked, I found myself being more playful, more spontaneous, less tethered to order for order's sake.

My thinking: That year said no over and over, so I tried to say yes as often as I could. Sometimes *yes* looked like ice cream for dinner or an '80s dance party in the living room or a water fight in the backyard past bedtime. Sometimes *yes* looked like a couple of middle-aged women roller-skating in a driveway.

Yes also looked like meeting someone when I least expected it—in those last weeks right before lockdown, when we were still able to go to coffeeshops and concerts. On the one hand, the timing could not have been worse; on the other, it could not have been better. Starting a new relationship in quarantine felt like growing a plant inside in a small terrarium. We tended to it in a protected environment before planting it outside and seeing how it might fare in the elements.

That July we drove eleven hours from Ohio to the North Carolina coast, just the two of us, our first trip together. After being cooped up and landlocked for months, we both desperately needed to see the ocean. The world felt so changed, part of me doubted it would still be there.

But it was there. I swam and bobbed in the waves, despite years of a reticence that bordered on fear. The thing about the ocean is that when you're in it, you're not in control; you can't even see what's moving all around you, beneath the surface. But this time, I wasn't afraid. We saw a pod of dolphins. We stepped, shrieking, on the same crab, one after the other, and laughed until we cried.

I didn't forget the global pandemic or my government's slide toward full-on fascism. I didn't leave behind the stresses of being self-employed or my concerns about keeping my children healthy—physically and mentally—during that time. But I let myself feel something *other* than all that.

What I want to remember about that time—and what I want my kids to remember—is unselfconscious joy, tenderness, and togetherness. I want them to remember that their mother was happy, not that she had dinner on the table at 6:00 every night, or that bedtime was always at 8:00. I want them to remember all the things we did, not the things we weren't able to do.

Sometimes *yes* looks like reminding yourself of what is still possible.

I went to find beauty, and it was still there. I go looking for it, and it's there.

SOME PEOPLE WILL ASK

"Why didn't you write more about [person x] or [event y]?"
    Maybe you consider it sleight of hand, a kind of lie, because I'm not giving you my whole life. Maybe you want me to explain.

—I could say I explained in the first sentence, the very first sentence, that this isn't a tell-all. Why, then, would you expect me to tell you everything? I could say this is a tell-mine, or maybe a find-mine, but it's also in part a keep-mine. I made specific choices about what to include in this book, so there are omissions and redactions, joys and sadnesses I didn't commit to these pages. No, I'm not saying much here about beginning a new relationship post-divorce. No, my sex life is not in this book, but believe me when I tell you that I enjoy several things more in middle age than I did when I was younger: naps, running, cooking, traveling, sex—

"A memoir is about 'the art of memory,' and part of the art is in the curation. This isn't the story of a woman who fell in love again and therefore was healed and lived happily ever after. This is the story of a woman coming home to *herself.*"
Next question.

I thought that I was vanishing, but instead
I was only coming true.

—Clive James

WHAT NOW, MOM?

That first pandemic fall my dining room was a second-grade classroom. My office was a middle school. On the first day of school, I cried twice. One was a good cry. The other was not so good. But my kids cried zero times. They were teaching me how to roll with it. Yes, on their first day of school, they were teaching me.

Our school district had been aiming for a hybrid model—two days a week in the classroom, socially distanced and masked, and three days virtual learning from home. But with coronavirus cases rising, and the largest school district opting for virtual learning for the first nine weeks, many other districts in our county followed suit. We knew the kids might have the option to be back in the classroom at some point during the school year, but they started the year at home.

Violet's sixth-grade classroom was my writing studio, a small room wrapped in windows. It's full of bookcases, my turntable, my records. I gave her a glass of water and a snack, and shut the French doors behind her. She opened her district-provided laptop, put on her headphones, and except for one quick break between classes, didn't emerge most days until lunch.

Meanwhile, Rhett and I sat together at the dining room table, which was covered with colored folders, workbooks, markers, crayons, and pencils. I lovingly called him my officemate.

On the second day of school, my officemate had to share three things he loves as a way to tell his classmates about himself. He shared his *Yellow Submarine* CD, his skateboard, and his old hardcover copy of *Black Beauty*. I listened in, grinning and making eye contact with him across the table, over my own open laptop, while I tried to catch up on email.

That day, during Rhett's twenty minutes of independent reading, the teacher asked the children to mute themselves on Zoom, go find a cozy place to read, and then return to their computers for the next lesson. My officemate was curled up in his favorite turquoise reading chair, his feet up on the ottoman.

From his laptop still open on the table across from me, I heard the tiny voice of a girl from his class who was unmuted: "What now, Mom?"

My heart caught in my throat.

"What now, Mom?" is what so many of us were hearing and feeling.

I've been self-employed since Violet was two, so working from home is what I do, pandemic or not. But I hadn't anticipated being a second-grade teacher's aide, in addition to freelance writing and editing, Zooming my book tour for *Keep Moving*, and teaching in an MFA program.

As challenging as this time was, I tried to see the hidden gifts—the ones tucked inside these big changes. One was being able to be a part of my children's school day. For the first few years they were in school, I walked them into their classrooms each morning and was able to see their cubbies, their class pets, their art and writing posted on the walls. I checked in with their teachers; I met the other parents.

So many school shootings later, the parent walk-in policy changed, and I was privy only to bits and pieces of their days—what they would tell me as we walked home from school, what the work in their take-home folders revealed, what I'd glean from teacher emails or school newsletters or parent-teacher conferences. But during lockdown, I lived in their school. I was sitting right there, listening along, helping find the right folder or workbook, keeping track of the time, making sure they were fed.

Was I stressed out because I couldn't work on those days, when normally I'd count on their schooltime as my work time? Yes. But that didn't negate the gifts.

My focus was, and is, on our health—both physical and mental. I was, and am, less concerned with the kids' schoolwork than with their well-being. So I praised their adaptability, their patience, their effort, their ability to make the best of a less-than-ideal situation. I praised myself for these things, too. And I tried to carve out space for joy and pleasure however and whenever I could.

We discovered the power of quick breaks—for a walk around the block with the dog, or Legos, or skateboarding for ten minutes before the next Zoom class. We ate our meals on a picnic blanket in the front yard for as long as weather allowed it. One day, the neighbor kids came over with their own lunches and their own blanket—plus some tomatoes warm from their garden—and the four of them had a socially distanced lunch on the lawn. They sat, ate, talked about their days. It was the closest thing possible to normal. But you know what? Maybe it was better than normal. I don't have fond memories of the middle school cafeteria, do you? A blanket in the sun with people you've known all your life, and no worries about where to sit and with whom? I'll take it.

While the weather was warm, we did as much schoolwork as we could outside, too. One day, Rhett's second-grade social studies work happened on a beach towel in the grass. He borrowed a clipboard from Violet, I cut him some apple slices and put them in a small plastic bowl, and we went out front to do his assignment: "Draw a picture of your family."

On the top of his paper, he drew the three of us: me, him, his sister. He added our dog, Phoebe. On the bottom half, he drew his father, him again, his sister again. Everyone was smiling.

BECAUSE I WAS A BEGGAR

A few months into the pandemic, after my road trip to the ocean, I had the first of three sessions via phone with an emotional alchemist. My friend Kelly, who would be the first to admit she's more "woo" than me, recommended her. I reached out to Kathryn to make an appointment, because what could it hurt? And hurting was the issue. I wanted to whittle my hurt down to something manageable—fun size instead of full size.

I didn't pray, though I'm quite sure others prayed on my behalf. I wished hard. I tried many things, because beggars can't be choosers. Yoga, reiki, aromatherapy. I went to a guided meditation class and felt myself floating around at the ceiling like a helium balloon that had slipped from a child's grasp. My friend Dawn took me to see a psychic. Kelly read my tarot cards. I smudged the house with a thick bundle of sage. I threw away most of what he left behind. I replaced the things we'd bought together, the mattress he'd slept on, the couch he'd slept on. I wrote as if writing could exorcise the experience. I ran as if *exercise* were a suitable alternative to *exorcise*.

The first time I spoke to Kathryn on the phone, it was for an initial consultation. I was sitting in an Adirondack chair in my backyard in the sunshine, scribbling notes on a yellow legal pad as she spoke. My kids were with their father for the weekend. Kathryn described emotional alchemy as being related to how we metabolize experience. She would be able to access the energy inside me, she said, and move it—shift it, clear it—if need be. *Yes, please*, I thought. The energy inside me felt heavy and dark and untitled, like Rothko's painting.

The second time we spoke, Kathryn began by asking to access my energy. She said she could feel the blockage—it was in my chest. The line was so staticky, I couldn't hear her, and she couldn't hear me clearly either. She said sometimes that happens when the energy is particularly strong, and she'd do some quick clearing and I could call back. We hung up. I waited a minute, breathing deeply to calm myself, and called her back. This time the line was completely clear. No, I can't explain that. And no, it doesn't matter, not really, if it was coincidence or if everything I was carrying—the black, the gray—interrupted the connection, a kind of electrical storm inside me. That clearing felt *true* even if now, in hindsight, I'm not sure it was *real*.

Once, while doing dishes in the kitchen, I overheard my kids bickering in the living room. Rhett, just three years old then, said, "Everything is true." And Violet asked, "Do you mean *real*?" Is there a difference? Some days I'm not sure if I would recognize either.

At the end of our conversation, Kathryn gave me a few tips for clearing bad energy myself. She suggested some things to buy and keep around the house, some mantras to repeat. And I tried. I tried all if it, even the witchiest things, because beggars can't be choosers, and because I was a beggar.

A NOTE ON PLOT

The way I see it, the inciting incident in this story had its own inciting incident, and that event had its own inciting incident, and another and another . . . all the way back to the beginning, when my story was my own, separate, because I hadn't even met the man I would marry. Back when I was *mine*. The inciting incidents of this story go back and back and back until they're just specks on the horizon. I can't even see them.

EMAIL, SUBJECT LINE: UPDATE

He is relocating out of state, sometime in the next few months. He's telling the kids today.

THIS IS WHERE I COMPLETELY FREAKED OUT

Reader, let's take a minute and unpack that email.

Did I panic? Yes.

Would you panic if your coparent, with whom you shared equal custody, announced in a businesslike email that he was moving approximately five hundred miles away? If the move was a personal choice, not a job transfer, not a deployment? If your children were in the middle of their second-grade and sixth-grade school years? If you were in the middle of a pandemic? If now the last court case that had dragged on for months would have to be rolled into a new one? (Spoiler alert: We would spend another year in litigation. Another full year, during a pandemic, while single parenting. Someone please cue the sound of cash register *cha-chinging*, then the sad trombone. *Womp womp womp*.)

Would you panic if you had no idea from this email what he intended to do? Was he going to try to take the kids? Did he plan on giving up custody?

Would you panic if you had no idea what he was telling the kids, that very day, because what the hell was the plan? And if you had no way to reach your kids except through him, and he wasn't allowing a phone call?

Did I panic? Yes. I lost my goddamn mind.

BUBBLES

During the first several months of the pandemic, my children traveled from one bubble to another, from one isolation to another isolation on the other side of town. Then, in December, three months after he coolly announced in an email that he was moving, he left the state, and he took his isolation with him.

A FRIEND SAYS EVERY
BOOK BEGINS WITH AN
UNANSWERABLE QUESTION

Then what is mine?
how to heal

KEEP MOVING

It was Violet's twelfth birthday. We were standing in the kitchen when she said, "I saw your book ad in the *New York Times*. We were wrapping the dishes in newspaper at Dad's, and there it was."

At our house, we were getting ready to celebrate her birthday. Across town her father was packing up a U-Haul trailer and heading east, a few states away. "Keep Moving," indeed. It was too on the nose. It was his third move in two years.

"At least there's no shortage of material!" I've told my mother/my friend/ my agent on the phone. "He's giving me plenty of material!" I've said, laughing, because if you don't laugh . . .

As if harm can be alchemized into something useful. The harm becomes material.

As my friend Cait said, "At least your terrible divorce wasn't wasted on someone who isn't a writer." I laughed. Maybe to write a memoir is to believe that. Maybe one must believe that to write a memoir. If one has the lemons, after all . . .

Violet was standing in my kitchen. A few blocks away, her father was moving nearly five hundred miles away on her birthday. He packed everything he owned. He left us plenty of material.

THINGS I KNOW FOR SURE

This isn't a tell-all. You can see that by now. I'm looking for answers, looking for the *mine*. There are things I'll never know, and I'm coming to terms with that fact. I accept it.

But I know this: I found a postcard in my husband's unmistakable handwriting, addressed to a woman in another city and state. I know this, too: on my daughter's twelfth birthday, her father moved to that city and state to live with that woman, 462 miles from the house we bought together when Violet was one. A fair amount of his mail still comes here, where it goes straight into the recycling.

I know this: He went from having a long-distance relationship with an adult to having a long-distance relationship with our children. I know this, but I don't understand it. I can't fathom it.

I know this: After their first visit to their father's new house, the week after Christmas, he dropped them off here with selfies and a box of self-addressed stamped postcards—things you might give to a teenage girl after a summer camp romance, hoping she might write. I thought immediately of the scene in Cameron Crowe's *Say Anything*, where John Cusack's character, Lloyd Dobler, is crying in a phone booth. He says into the phone, "I gave her my heart and she gave me a pen."

So now my children are supposed to be pen pals with their own father? It's not enough. It's less than they deserve.

I don't know the whole story, so I can't give it to you. Even if I knew the whole story, I wouldn't hand you all of it. But there are a few things I know for sure. My children have a box of postcards addressed to their father in another state. Yes, postcards.

THE SPARKS

That part about being pen pals? I wrote that with sparks in my hair. I wrote it from inside the blue part of a flame, and then I thought about removing it. I'm trying so hard to forgive. I'm wishing hard for peace in every superstitious way. Wishing for it deep inside me, where the truest things live.

In the end, I let it stand. *Stet*, as we write when we don't want our words changed. I let it stand because I'm trying to tell you the truth. My truth. I'm trying to show you my hands, even when my hands are burning.

A HALF HOUR TO CRY

"I just need to find a half hour to cry." I was sitting in my office, in the middle of a virtual therapy session. I don't think I'll ever forget the look on my therapist's face when I said that. The way she raised her hand to her forehead.

I began therapy right after my children's father moved. Scheduling sessions with Megan, like scheduling calls with my lawyer, was difficult. I couldn't do either with my kids in the house. At that time, because school was hybrid and their father had moved away, I had only two and a half hours twice a week with no one else here. Five hours total alone each week. I insisted I was fine. For more than a year, I'd insisted I was fine. I was not fine.

How did I take care of my mental health before therapy? I poured myself into writing *Keep Moving*. I took long walks with my headphones on. I started running. I had one-woman dance parties in my kitchen. I planned many, many happy hours and not-so-happy hours with friends, unpacking the hardest parts of my life, unpacking and unpacking and unpacking. At least one bearded bartender probably knows my story very well. My next-door neighbor, gardening on the other side of the "privacy" fence, has heard it all, I'm sure—the backyard talks, the tearful phone calls, the aggravated calls with my lawyer as I paced in the grass.

As a self-employed writer, I didn't—and don't—have good health insurance, so I knew I would have to pay out of pocket to talk to someone, but I could talk to my mom, my sisters, and my friends for free! For free and often over drinks and snacks! Still, I wanted to be able to talk about other things with my friends over drinks and snacks. I didn't want to be *that friend*—the one you know that when you see them and ask "How are you?" they will tell you how the fuck they are and it is not good, people. I worried about grinding people down on the sparking wheel of my divorce. Because if you talked to me on a Monday, by Wednesday there were developments. Hold my beer, life seemed to say.

I knew that after the children's father moved away, I would need more than DIY therapy. I would need the real thing—a place to put all of it, so the people I loved best wouldn't be constantly subjected to the worst of me. I was shocked (again), angry (again), sad (again), and worried (again), but this time it was worse, because I was feeling these things more for my kids than for myself. I found Megan, my therapist, through a dear friend who's been seeing her for years.

During our first session, she asked, simply, "How are you doing?"

"We're hanging in there," I told her. I talked about how the kids were coping, how they were communicating more, how I was managing their schedules on my own.

She let me finish, and then she asked again. "No, how are *you* doing? What are you doing to take care of *yourself*?"

That's when I said it. I just needed to find a free half hour so I could cry. A friend posted on social media around that time: *How many moms are crying in bathrooms?* I think moms crying in bathrooms during the pandemic could be a coffee-table book. A very thick coffee-table book.

A NOTE ON BETRAYAL

've said it before: Betrayal is neat. Except when it's not.

I was processing my own sense of betrayal—I was a grown-up, I could figure it out—but when he moved, I felt that he betrayed the kids. Broke his unspoken, unwritten, but still-real and still-solemn vows to them. And that hurt worse.

In the email announcing his move, subject line *Update*, he called me "Mag." My reply—before I lost my goddamn mind—began, "First, don't call me Mag."

Mag is what my mother calls me. Mag is what my friend Lesley calls me, and I call her Lu. Mag is for family, blood and chosen. If you hurt me or the people I love, you don't get to call me Mag.

AN OFFERING

The Little Red Hen was a favorite bedtime story book when my kids were younger. My favorite illustration in our copy shows the hen's face reflected in a cake knife. She asks for help over and over—planting the seeds, harvesting the wheat, milling the flour, and finally baking the cake—but no one will help. Her refrain, every time she asks and they refuse to pitch in: "Then I shall have to do it myself."

Tell me about it, Hen.

Now I can't think about this story without thinking about the torma. I've thought so much about forgiveness, and I'm trying. I've baked the cake—this is it—and I'm offering it to you.

GRENADE

It makes me feel a little seasick to think about it now: Week after week in marriage counseling we focused on my work, and specifically my occasional travel, because I waited so long to tell the therapist about the postcard and the notebook. After we stopped going to counseling, I wondered: *Why didn't I bring that up right away? It was the reason we started therapy! Why did I hold that huge piece of the puzzle out of view? Why didn't I show her my hands, the heft of what I was carrying?*

I understand now: I was afraid. I didn't want to anger or upset him. I wanted to save the marriage, as if I held a grenade in my trembling hands, barely daring to breathe, and just prayed I wouldn't jostle it and set it off. To tell the truth was to pull the pin.

WOLF IN SHEEP'S CLOTHING

"At least with a conservative Republican guy, you know what you're getting," my friend Kelly said. "You can opt in or opt out."

We were in her car, driving the two hours from Athens, Ohio, back to Columbus, after picking up her teenage son from a weekend visit with his father. He was in the backseat.

"But the guy who's all left-leaning, even calls himself a feminist, but then he expects you to handle everything at home and doesn't want to work around your career at all—that's a wolf in sheep's clothing," she said.

I knew what she meant: the man who considers himself progressive, but when it comes down to the division of labor in the home, not so much.

"Maybe I wasn't particularly good at being a wife?" I said. I've been trying to self-interrogate, to hold myself accountable for the marriage we built together, both of us, over years and years. "Maybe I wasn't really suited for it?" But I don't believe that's true. I think I could be a good partner in a different kind of partnership.

I wasn't good at being the version of myself I needed to be in my marriage. I wasn't good at handling what was, apparently, "the deal." Was the deal that we'd both freeze at the instant of "I do" and not grow or change or succeed or fail or suffer or triumph from that day forward, till death do us part? Or was the deal that he could grow and change, choosing a new career entirely, an incredibly demanding career, and that I would have to put my own dreams on hold because I made less money? Was that the deal?

Kelly and I talked the whole way to my house, the landscape gradually flattening as we left the hills of southern Ohio and entered the middle of the state, the heart of the heart. We agreed: "The deal" should be that both people get to be themselves and do their work. If I respected you and your work, I wouldn't begrudge you the time and space it takes to do it. If you respected me and my work, you wouldn't begrudge me the time and space to do it, either.

If, if, if.

~~SAD-ASS~~ DIVORCE DREAM

I dreamed I was sitting at a table beside my children's father, and his mother sat across from us. The woman wasn't his actual mother, but one of those stand-ins the subconscious often employs. In the dream, his mother-not-mother owned a successful bookstore, but he was belittling her business. He said something about market value, and she was visibly wounded. His tone of voice was cold and critical. I knew that tone of voice.

I stood up from my chair, leaned down, and yelled right in his ear: *You are not a good person! I felt sorry for you, but not anymore. I'm done with you.*

Then I woke up.

WHEN IT RAINS, IT POURS

My lawyer and my dentist retired in the same month. If you knew how much I'd been grinding my teeth because of the divorce you'd understand why this was a problem. My night mouth guard looked like it was found in the middle of a highway. I'd cracked a filling.

My case would be handled by a different lawyer at the firm, and I'd have to get him up to speed. I'd also need to find a new dentist. I'd chipped two of my bottom teeth. When I concentrated hard—working on a poem, thinking through how to respond to a difficult email or text—I ran my tongue along the rough edges.

ABOUT THE BODY

In January, about a year into the pandemic, I went back to my doctor. Right before Christmas, my arrhythmia started acting up again, more intensely than it had since I was pregnant. I could feel my heart skip a beat, then kick in harder, and I'd cough to shake the feeling, like I was trying to clear my heart from my throat. In a pandemic where one of the common symptoms is a dry cough, you really don't want to be coughing in public because of palpitations.

I wasn't going to call my GP, but it began happening more and more. It kept me up at night. It felt like someone was driving stick shift in my chest but hadn't learned how to use the clutch yet. Finally it got so frequent and severe that I could hear when it happened on recordings. I listened to a podcast I'd been a guest on, and I could hear when it happened—the air forced out, interrupting my speech, and then the cough. For weeks I coughed—or tried to hold my breath—through online readings and workshops and meetings with my graduate students.

Finally I made the appointment—*heart trouble*, I told the receptionist—and went to see my doctor the following week. (Yes, the same doctor who asked me if I needed an STD test when I told him I was getting divorced.) The EKG was normal, as I'd expected, because I hadn't felt my heart skipping for several days before the visit. Isn't that always the way? But I'd bought a pulse oximeter; it was one of those things you were supposed to have on hand in case someone in your household got Covid. You could test their oxygen levels and know whether or not they needed to go to the hospital.

My oxygen levels were fine, but I took video on my iPhone of my finger in the device, and I could see my pulse, like a seismograph, each beat a little mountain, each space between a valley. I could also see my heart skipping beats and coming back late and strong—it registered as long, flat pauses followed by a taller peak. I showed my doctor the video after the EKG came back normal, to show him that I wasn't imagining it. Of course I wasn't imagining it.

He asked if something had happened in mid-December that might explain the palpitations returning. Increased stress, perhaps?

Yes, I said. Yes.

It hadn't even registered with me until that moment: My children's father had moved away in mid-December.

The doctor said my prognosis is good. My heart is strong, and usually it plays its song just fine, but sometimes it skips like a scratched record. An "electrical" issue, nothing dangerous, he said.

My trigger is stress, so my treatment is perspective.

I'M ALL YOURS

One night that winter, Rhett was being a little grumpy and stubborn in the window of time between dinner and bed. He was tired, but he was also carrying a lot. His father had moved away the month before, and that absence weighed—*weighs*—more than I can imagine. It's the elephant, not the elephant's shadow.

I told Rhett, "I'm all yours," meaning in that moment we could do whatever he wanted to do—a board game, a book, modeling clay, charades, Legos, cards, an art project—but also, beyond that, I'm right here, always, no matter what. I saw his face soften, and then he smiled. What did he want? A bowl of apple slices and for me to snuggle up and read *Calvin and Hobbes* to him. Done and done.

That night when I tucked him in, he said, "I'm all yours, too." We curled up together in his bed, and I rested my head on his chest, the way he's done with me for years. I could hear the clock of his heart right under my ear. If there's a better way to keep time, I don't know it.

FATHOMED

My mind runs constantly. If I'm quiet and still, I can almost hear the old-appliance hum of it. Maybe you can hear it as you turn these pages. Is that whir the sound of rumination? The mind chewing and chewing on a thing, unable to swallow?

I worry about money, work, relationships. I worry about the future, which seems shrouded in dense fog. What will materialize out of it that I can't yet see? But mostly I worry about my kids. What are they thinking, feeling, absorbing? What are they carrying? I can't imagine what it would feel like to have a parent choose to move so far away. It's still unfathomable to me. *Fathom* from the Old English, meaning "outstretched arms." Once the verb *fathom* meant to encircle something with your arms as if to measure it. Once *fathom* was a synonym for "embrace."

Looking at the word *fathom*, you might think it shares a root with the word *father*. It doesn't.

I have to trust this: If what I give my children is love, then they're receiving it. If I seek to understand them, then they will feel understood. Embraced. Fathomed.

AN OFFERING

I've been thinking more about the don. I've been thinking that I've become a student of my own pain, my own grief and suffering. In this way, he has been my teacher?

He has been my teacher.

THIS MOMENT ISN'T FOR YOU

It was a January night, there was a coup in the capital, and there were tears in our house at bedtime. Is it enough for me to tell you this, or do you want me to show you? Reader, ask yourself: Why would you want to see someone else's children crying? My children aren't characters in a novel or a movie or a play, they're real, and their grief is real, so this moment isn't for you.

That night Violet said something that snapped a piece of my heart clean off. I won't write it here. For a while I carried it inside me like a small, sharp thing that cut me when I moved wrong. As I lay beside her in her twin bed, I told her that when she was a toddler, maybe two years old, I slept with her in the guest room—now her brother's bedroom—one winter night. She was sick with the flu, and I didn't want her to be alone, so we curled up in that big bed together. I told her that when she and Rhett were babies, I'd sleep on the floor beside their cribs if they had coughs or fevers. "God, the floor was so hard," I said, jokingly showing her how I'd toss and turn all night, and we laughed.

After I tucked her in, I went back downstairs, emotionally exhausted, and finished the dinner dishes. I moved the clean, wet laundry from the washer to the dryer. I let the dog out one last time into the backyard, then crated her for the night in her small doghouse beside my desk. I went to bed, and every time I rolled over I swore I could feel the sharp thing inside me, so I tried to lie very still.

TELL-MINE

've wondered if I can even call this book a *memoir*. It's not something that happened in the past that I'm recalling for you. It's not a recollection, a retrospective, a reminiscence. I'm still living through this story as I write it. I'm finding mine, and telling it, but all the while, the mine is changing.

THE ARCHIVE I HAVE

keep thinking about what I know and what I don't, what I remember and what I've lost. I kept a baby book for Violet, and a wall calendar that came with stickers for milestones: *first solid food, rolled over, first tooth*. Rhett? Neither. This is so often the lot of the second child. What have I forgotten? How much of their childhood is lost?

I searched my old social media posts for the kids' names to find the bits of daily life with young children—the moments of sweetness or exhaustion or fear, the funny things they said. This is the archive I have, like an album of Polaroids I can flip through and remember.

December 5, 2011
This morning, Violet declared her stuffed Clifford the Big Red Dog to be, and I quote, "a casual genius."

January 18, 2012
Violet, while we were doing a puzzle this morning: "Mom, can I have you forever?"

March 27, 2014
Last night my dream involved losing track of Rhett at a house party, and then finding that he had left out the back door, toddled through the yard and across a stream into some tenement with broken glass and nails everywhere. Clearly I'm having some anxiety about starting him in daycare two days a week in May.

October 22, 2014

At Trader Joe's tonight:

Violet (in her hot-pink sparkly boots): "I'm cool today, and you're plain."

Me (in my beloved, beat-up gray Chucks): "I love these shoes. They've been around so long, they're part of the family."

Violet: "No they're not. They're not funny, and they don't love you."

I love this definition of family: funny people who love you. Truth.

December 15, 2014

I seriously can't get over Rhett's first-person/third-person meta-dialogue: "I WANT MORE JUICE, Rhett said." He's like a two-year-old Bob Dole who's been read A LOT of books. The last few days he's been talking about himself like he's a book character.

April 16, 2015

Rhett, eating his lunch: "I love you more than the moon and the sun."

Me: [taking off my glasses, wiping tears away]

Rhett: "Don't be sad, Mom. Don't be scared. Put your glasses on. I love you."

September 24, 2015

I bought Violet a felt raccoon key chain at Wholly Craft tonight. She named it Darkness. On the drive home, I heard her whisper, "Darkness, look away from the light!"

March 3, 2016

This morning I told Violet, my seven-year-old, that I know I had a dream last night but couldn't quite remember it. She said, "Like a hawk circling your head."

August 2, 2016

When Rhett stopped saying "alligator" for "elevator" I died a little.

But at the beach he's been calling the cormorants "coroners" and I am so happy.

December 21, 2016

Rhett ran into our room this morning and shouted, "What're ya doing? Just laying in bed like whores?" He then told us that a whore is a kind of rabbit.

Hare. We were lying in bed as cozy as hares. I have never laughed harder before being fully awake.

January 31, 2017

Rhett today: "I don't like feeling sick, but I love when you take care of me. You're the sweetest best mommy, and your tummy feels like a squishy puffball."

I was all smiles until that last bit. Then I all-out laughed.

SOME PEOPLE ASK

"Do you think the divorce made your kids more resilient?" I have been asked this question, and I have bitten the insides of my cheeks bloody to avoid answering plainly.

—I could say their father said that once, that they'd be more resilient. I could say how angry I was about that, as if the divorce were a gift we were giving them, as if this were a kind of bootcamp, running through tires and army-crawling through mud and hauling themselves over a wall. As if you have to break someone's heart to make them strong. I could say you don't get to take credit for someone's growth if they grow as a result of what you put them through. I could say you don't get to gouge out a child's eyes and then marvel at how keen their hearing is now. I could say you don't get to crush a child's legs and then praise them for how still they can sit. I could say you don't get to cut a child's hands off at the wrist and then exclaim, proudly, "Look, they can write with their feet!" I could say what I want to say in two words, which are "Fuck resilience"—

"Are the kids more resilient now? Maybe they are. But what kind of trade-off is that?" Next question.

BECAUSE YOU CAN'T MISPLACE YOUR EARLOBE

When my son misses me, he rubs one of his velvety earlobes. It started in kindergarten, when the kids were first bouncing back and forth between two houses: a few days here, a few days there. Rhett's father had given him a trinket of some kind—a lucky coin stamped with a four-leaf clover, if I'm remembering it right. It was something Rhett could hold when he missed him. But what could he take to his father's house for comfort when he missed me?

Trinkets get lost, I thought. I remembered the stuffed animals I bought in pairs when Violet was little—two pink bunnies, two Sweet Pea dolls—in case one was lost or left in a cubby at daycare or just in the wash. So I suggested his earlobe. Whenever he rubs it, he knows I'm somewhere thinking of him.

HIDDEN VALENTINES

I found a small white heart cut from paper on the photograph of seven-year-old me in my Brownie uniform. On it: *i love you.* I found one inside my laptop: *i miss you.* One in the bread box, one in the netted bag of mandarin oranges, one on the bookshelf in the dining room. It was the weekend of my birthday and Valentine's Day, and the kids were visiting their father out of state, so Rhett left little love notes for me to find while they were gone. Outside, snow accumulated, enveloped, obscured, buried, softened the edges of things or crystallized around them. Time did these things, too. I was alone, but the house was full of hidden valentines.

How I picture it: That life—the past, the beforelife, the beforemath—was a boat. The life I lived after, the afterlife, was on an island. I was marooned. I watched the horizon for sails. I wasted so much time, sunrise to sunset, thinking about the boat and what had been moving, slowly, darkly, in the water beneath it—time I could have been collecting rainwater or weaving leaves into shelter.

Some nights were so overcast, I wondered if there had ever been stars. Other nights, lying on my back, I could see so many stars, anything felt possible.

A FRIEND SAYS EVERY BOOK BEGINS WITH AN UNANSWERABLE QUESTION

Then what is mine?
how to live with the mystery

HOME

Tonight, getting ready for bed—after taking my melatonin gummy, after telling Alexa to play rain sounds on a loop—it hits me: *My children have a vacation home.*

BITTERSWEET

In March, the kids traveled to their father's house for spring break. Rhett hid little notes for me again, this time shaped like tiny butterflies. The day they left, I saw a yellow paper butterfly behind my phone charger: *i miss you*. I found another one the next day, while putting my hat and gloves away in a drawer: *i love you mom*. Yes, I cried. I cried and rubbed my earlobe.

That week, while they were gone, I went back to southeastern Ohio to write for a few days. Once, many Marches ago, a deer came right up to the side of the cabin, eating the tender early grasses that came up after the thaw. My husband took its picture from the window.

I was back there again, in our happy place, which is still my happy place. This time, I wrote for three days, all day long. I took breaks to walk the dog, my headphones on, listening to a new playlist: Waxahatchee, M. Ward, Fruit Bats, Andy Shauf, The National. I took long baths. I watched twilight descend, turning the trees into black construction paper cutouts. Each morning I woke early and walked down to pick up breakfast and coffee to go from the inn's restaurant, and squirreled it back to my cabin. I ate the same breakfasts my husband and I used to eat together, sat in the same chairs we used to sit in, turned the fireplace on to hear the familiar *whoosh* of the gas igniting and the clicking of the timer switch on the wall.

There are so many things about time I will never understand. They say, "You never step in the same river twice." (Just then I typed *over* instead of *river*, and that, too, is true: you never step in the same *over* twice. The over-ness endures but is different, somehow, always.)

I'd grabbed an old, half-full legal pad from my office to bring with me, and in the cabin I flipped back to the beginning, to the first page, dated eight years earlier. Rhett is a baby, just about a year old, and Violet is in pre-K at the JCC. Each classroom has a name: Teddy Bears, Crocodiles, the Rainbow Room. She's in the Dragonfly Room with her teacher, Miss Carol. There's a list of jobs on the bulletin board in her classroom, which the kids rotate through:

line leader, bell ringer, lunch helper, and my favorite, dragonfly wrangler. Violet has just learned to zip her own coat—she's in the "zipper club," says Miss Carol, and we all make a big fuss about it. Being in the zipper club means she no longer needs me for this one thing, and many other things will follow.

On the next page, from the same year: notes from a freelance meeting, the launch of a big elementary reading project for an educational publisher. Violet is in part-time preschool, and Rhett is home with me every day. He won't start part-time daycare for another few months. During this time I'm taking on as much freelance work as I can. I'm working while Violet is at school; working while Rhett naps, *if* Rhett naps; working at night after the kids go to bed, sometimes very late; I'm working on weekends when their father is around to help out. In other words, I'm working during the hours when the kids don't need me.

On the next page: a list of items to sell on the neighborhood for-sale page, a social media group of mostly moms making extra cash on the side selling hand-me-downs washed in free and clear detergent, or old baby toys, or snow boots their kid outgrew after wearing them once. Most items have a price listed, then OBO: *or best offer.* On my list: baby stuff, clothes Rhett has outgrown, toys that no longer catch his eye. *Inflatable baby tub, size 5 baby shoes, lacing beads, bottles, magnet dolls.*

I flip to the next page and find notes I jotted down about Violet's preschool field trip to the Ohio Historical Society. *The large brown bat, taxidermied. A glass case full of dissected owl pellets, the tiny skulls inside as delicate as sea shells.*

We saw a great horned owl, she says. *It was dead.*

Guess what the great horned owl that was dead said?

What?

Nothing.

When I flip the page again, I spring forward seven years—notes I scrawled during a call from my lawyer, that first pandemic summer. I must have grabbed the nearest pad of paper I could find and flipped to the first blank page. I see the word *interrogatories.* The question *What do they want?* is circled once, twice, my pen containing the question. My pen was *penning* the question, it occurs to me now. Fencing it in.

And this is life, page after page. One life. Zippers and owls and dolls with magnetic dresses. Lawyers and bills and colder words for *questions.*

I keep finding these half-full legal pads and notebooks around my house, and in them so much life I'd forgotten. Pieces that would have stayed lost: Rhett hissing *sssssss* for "sissy," what he called Violet. Me cutting a few curls out of his eyes, just a few locks, sandwich bagged. The times I galloped him across the preschool parking lot, and he squealed, holding my face in both hands, and kissed me, murmuring *mamamamama*.

Is this why we write? To bronze the baby shoes? To save all of it? The zippered coats, the somehow endless buckling and unbuckling of car seat harnesses, the sticky hands, the fought naps, the acorns secreted into my pockets and purses, the crumbs on everything, always?

Looking at the first pages in this legal pad, basking in the bright and often painful light of hindsight, I see something—*someone*—missing on those pages. Even then, I wrote the three of us, a unit—a mother and her two children. We three. I wrote from the daily experience of mothering them. But how strange to see this now, on a legal pad, when we three is all there is in this house? *All there is* meaning less than they deserve. Less than they deserve but all I have to give.

WELL, HE SHOULD KNOW

When I tell my poet-friend Barbara about the children's father moving out of state, she writes back: "Is that legal?"

(I am large, I contain multitudes.)
            —Walt Whitman

BUT HERE'S THE THING, WALT

Sometimes I'm tired of my multitudes.

How I picture it: The Big Bang just continues. The harm is not in the past. It, too, is ongoing. Everything is inching away from everything else, but not fast enough. The universe is not expanding fast enough.

AN OFFERING

My children's father has taught me many lessons, painfully, and the pain has changed me.

I want to become a different kind of student.

To be a different kind of student, I need a new teacher.

MORE SAD-ASS DIVORCE DREAMS, OR THE LITTLE RED HEN IN REVERSE

I dreamed the whole downstairs of the house was flooded—more than six inches of standing water, wasps floating in it, trash, some of our things. I went downstairs to survey the damage.

Someone asked, *Do you need some help?*

No, I've got it.

I went down into the basement—where there was even more water—for the shop vac, which I've never used in waking life and had never used before in the dream. I started sucking up the water, a little bit at a time. I told everyone else to stay upstairs safely out of the way, but they kept yelling down, *Are you sure we can't do anything?*

It was like trying to drain a pond with a drinking straw. It was useless, and I think I knew it, but I kept at it.

No, I've got it, I've got it.

Then I woke up.

THE SLIDESHOW

A couple of days after I dreamed the house was flooded, Rhett came home from school with a bag of microwave popcorn taped to a checklist for a parent. He'd made a slide presentation for his second-grade science research project about an animal. He'd chosen black rhinos. He'd worked on it on his own at school each day, and all I'd seen so far were drawings he was working on—drawings his teacher later scanned. That night we were supposed to watch his presentation and check off the necessary slides—introduction, life cycle, food, threats, fun facts—as we watched. There were also some lines for writing comments at the bottom.

I popped the popcorn and poured it into two bowls, filling a third bowl with butter-flavored puffs (basically salty, powdery Styrofoam packing peanuts) for Violet, because she couldn't eat popcorn then. Braces.

Violet and I sat down together on the couch, and Rhett set up his laptop on a side table, next to a bowl of popcorn, and started clicking through his slides, reading what he'd written for each one. I loved it—the drawings, the second-grade spelling of words, the choice of facts he thought were most interesting. The last slide was titled "about the author." It was a picture of my son in his classroom, masked, that his teacher had obviously taken, with a third-person bio he'd written about himself. "He lives in Bexly, Ohio, with his mom, sister, and dog."

My heart crumpled in my chest, but I couldn't let him—or his sister—see it. The family he described sounded small, smaller than I'd thought of it myself. What would his bio have said a year ago? That he lives sometimes in one house, sometimes in another?

Later that night, when we curled up to watch a movie, Violet and Rhett were snuggled up on either side of me, as usual, Phoebe wedged in with us, too. We call it "the dogpile." At bedtime, Rhett held on tight to me and buried his face in my neck.

I said, "I'm so proud to be your mom."

He said, "I'm so proud to be your son."

How I picture it: A scar tells a story about pain, injury, healing. Years, too, are scars.

The year their father moved away. Second grade, sixth grade. The year of Covid and masks and hand sanitizer. The year of unemployment and continued litigation. The year of Keep Moving. *The year I was tattooed with a gardenia, my mother's favorite flower. It was a beautiful and terrible year. Not but—and.*

The next year of more Covid and more litigation. Third grade, seventh grade. The year of Goldenrod *and the goldenrod tattoo. The year of Rilke written on a yellow sticky note, pressed to one of my office windows, referred to daily: "Let everything happen to you: beauty and terror. Just keep going. No feeling is final."*

A NOTE ON THE AUTHOR'S INTENTION

I wish to forgive, so this is aspirational. I write this aspirationally.

The way you'll be remembered is the way you're living now, I tell myself. If you don't like it, change it.

By the time these pages are printed, by the time you're reading this, may I be in a place of forgiveness.

NOSTALGIA

I'd been scrolling old pictures on my phone looking for something in particular—I can't remember what now—and found some photos of Rhett when he was only three years old. In one, he'd scribbled all over his face with a blue pen. I held up my phone to show him, and we giggled. The next one was a selfie, so I was in it. We're standing side by side in our aprons in the kitchen, smiling, snuggled up together to fit in the frame.

"We must have been baking that day," I said.

"I wish I could go back to that time," Rhett said. "Things were easier."

He was eight when he said that. Eight.

The *nost* in *nostalgia* means "homecoming"; the *algia* means "pain." Hundreds of years ago, nostalgia was a diagnosable medical condition. Johannes Hofer, a seventeenth-century Swiss physician, named the condition, which he identified in homesick soldiers. Symptoms of nostalgia among Swiss soldiers included melancholy, malnutrition, sleepiness, brain fever, and hallucinations.

THE PLAY

Before the play begins, somewhere offstage, somewhere unwritten, before The Wife becomes The Finder, before The Wife even becomes The Wife, she watches a play. How's that for meta?

The Not-Yet-Wife watches a play and doesn't see the foreshadowing. Dramatic irony is the last thing on her mind, because she doesn't know she'll marry the playwright. She doesn't know what will happen next . . . or what will happen next . . . or what will happen next . . .

Dot dot dot.

If there were a chorus in the play, like in a Greek tragedy, and if the chorus warned The Not-Yet-Wife that the marriage would become a cliché . . . that the divorce would be a cliché . . .

Dot dot dot.

The Not-Yet-Wife wouldn't believe the chorus. She wouldn't believe that someday she'd become The Finder. *We're writers*, she'd think. *Surely we could write a better story than that. Surely a poet and playwright could tell a more original story than that.*

A PANTOUM, A VILLANELLE, A GHAZAL

Living in Ohio my whole life, in the heart of the heart, and living in the same house where we once lived together, is like living inside a repetitive poem—a pantoum, a villanelle, a ghazal. There are always words and lines repeating, carrying forward, insisting on themselves.

On the way to the NPR station to record an audiobook, I passed my wedding venue. I parked in the parking lot shared by the NPR station and the wedding venue, and then I went inside to record the book I wrote during our divorce.

On the way to my lawyer's office, I passed the restaurant where we had our wedding rehearsal meal, and I passed the house where we lived when Violet was born. I parked there.

On the way to a gallery to pick up a painting I bought, I passed the flower shop where we bought our wedding flowers. New name, new ownership, but still there.

On the way to the dentist, I pass the pediatric dermatologist's office. I remember Violet dropping her first beloved doll, Sweet Pea, which she pronounced "Swippy," on the sidewalk outside, and a man called out to us and handed it back.

On the way to the pizza place, I pass the marriage counselor's office.

On the way to Schiller Park for a picnic, I pass the church where we always bought our Christmas trees. On the drive home, the tree tied to the roof of the car, I'd look up to see its branches through the sunroof.

On the way to the soccer stadium, I pass the apartment we lived in on September 11, 2001.

On the way to the record store, I pass the gallery where we had my second book party, and he stood onstage to introduce me.

In all these places, I loved that person. I loved him. Where does that go?

The love is in all of these places—haunting?—and in none of them. The love is everywhere and nowhere.

DISPOSABLE

I found a box of undeveloped disposable cameras in the basement, the kind with a little wheel you wind with your thumb until it clicks. The cameras must have been from the early 2000s, before we had smartphones, before all our pictures were of our children.

I unspooled a trash bag from the box under the kitchen sink, filled it with plastic cameras, and carried the bag to the trash in the alley behind my house. I will never see those photos, those faces, but I can imagine them: the two of us smiling on beaches or at house parties or in front of a Christmas tree. It was just the two of us back then.

There are so many images I can't access now, stories I can't tell and retell, because the person who was there isn't here. He made himself disappear. How did he *do* that?

This is something I grieve: the severed tie to someone who knew me since college, the cokeeper of our memories, the person who could tell my kids what I was like during those years, the person who could tell me what I was like, the person I shared my life with. All of it, disposable.

The same week I threw out the cameras, the kids and I went to get frozen custard in Clintonville, the neighborhood north of The Ohio State University where their father and I had lived together for years. Walking down an alley, I looked up and realized where we were—in front of the house where my husband and I lived the year after we were married. "That was our bedroom," I said, pointing to the second-story window at the front of the house. I didn't say: *The neighbors were drug-addled and violent, and we had to break our lease to move.*

On the drive home, we passed the apartment complex on Neil Avenue where we lived in my last year of graduate school, and then, a few blocks away, the half-double on Arcadia Avenue where we lived the year we were married. We wrote our wedding vows together on the front porch.

There is so much history here in Ohio, in the heart of the heart—so much shared history we carry separately now. He doesn't pass these landmarks from our years together every day, but I do. I still live in one of them.

Do those memories warp without their mirrors, without someone to reflect them, to keep them true, to show them their twin? Do our separate memories grow on their own into two different things, unrecognizable to one another? Do we?

GHOST STORY

We're living in a different kind of afterlife now. The afterlife, like the *mine* in *tell-mine*, keeps changing.

When people ask how the kids are doing since their father's move, I say, *Given the circumstances, they're doing great.* I say, *We're rallying.* I say, *They're incredible kids who are incredibly loved.*

How am I doing? On the bright side, there are fewer goodbyes now. I'm letting time work its magic. The house is not so haunted.

JACKPOT

Violet and I were walking together in our neighborhood. It was a virtual school day for her, but Rhett was in person, so I convinced her to walk a couple of blocks to the elementary school with me to pick him up.

"You hit the jackpot with your brother," I told her. "If you had to have an eight-year-old brother, which I know isn't always easy or fun, at least it's him and not some kid who just burps all the time and grunts about football and video games." She chuckled. "He's artistic and funny and smart. And he hit the jackpot with you, because it can't always be easy or fun to have a sister in middle school, but you're *you*. You're amazing."

She smiled over at me. "Well, good people make good people," she said, patting me on the back.

It was all I could do to say thank you without crying in front of the elementary school, because by that time we were there—we'd crossed at the crosswalk, on the side of the school where the hornet's nest had been the year before, and the fire department had come and blasted it away with the hose, but you could still see a gray shadow there. We were walking up to the front doors, and any minute the school nurse or music teacher would prop the door, and Rhett's teacher would lead the kids outside.

I hit the jackpot.

ON SECOND THOUGHT

've been thinking about what I said before, about wanting to undo it all. The more time that passes, the less I feel that way. Rilke comes to me in these moments, whispering, "No feeling is final."

I don't just want to have kids, I want *these* kids. Though dammit, I wish they had an easier path to travel. I wish we all had an easier path.

Here's what I think about the most: In some parallel universe, I can save the children and jettison the marriage. This is magical thinking. As in some Greek myth we're yet to discover, a son and daughter spring from me, whole.

WHEN THE METAPHOR IS RIGHT THERE

In second grade Rhett began reading a series of books called *Beast Quest*. He came home from a holiday visit at his father's house out of state with a box set, and when he tore through those I bought him the second set. One night, cuddled up together in his bed, the dog lying beside us like just another human, her head on a pillow, Rhett read part of one to me and told me the gist of the quest. A boy's father was cursed, turned into a ghost in some faraway land. The boy has to gather pieces of a missing amulet, and with each piece he finds, his father becomes more human, more in-the-flesh, less an apparition. The catch: The boy has been given his father's powers for this quest, and with every piece of the amulet he finds, the power leeches from the boy back to his father. It is a story about trying to save someone far away and losing parts of yourself in the process. It is a selfless story, a brave story, and the hero is the child.

ICARUS FLEW BEFORE HE FELL

Sometimes I wonder what my adult children will tell their therapists, assuming they'll have therapists. It's all conjecture.

Sometimes I want to tell them: I've tried to love you the right way.

I've tried to love them as if there is a right way. No, I've loved them without having to try at all, because I'm their mother, and the love is not work. *Parenting* is work: the cooking of meals, the washing of clothes, the tending of wounds, the taming of cowlicks, the helping with homework, the driving to soccer, the packing of lunches, the finding of missing things (water bottle lids, baseballs, library books, mittens), the consoling to sleep. The love? It's not work.

Sometimes I wonder: Who would they have been without the divorce, the pandemic, the move? What tenderness might be alive in them? What trust, what optimism, what confidence?

All wax and feathers, a mess of hope.

ABOUT THE BODY

I want to forgive, but first I need to feel everything that stands between me and forgiveness. Even my therapist notices: I can use the vocabulary—I can say I'm angry or anxious or sad—but I don't seem to *be* any of these things. She has a point. I don't walk around screaming, as my sister claimed she would if she were me, and I rarely cry. Am I *feeling* or simply describing feelings? Am I in my body or somehow out of it, like those Olan Mills photographs from my childhood: There's me looking right at the camera, head-on, and there's the faded-out profile of my face hovering just over my left shoulder.

How I picture it: My mind—my soul?—is an invisible balloon on an invisible string, tied to me, batting about in the air above me.

Because memory can't possibly live in the body, the way the mind cannot possibly live in the body—but where does it live? How is it tethered to me if not inside me?

Maybe this is what living is: trusting the string to hold. Trusting it not to float off, as if a child has let go, as if the loop knotted around her wrist at the fair has come loose, and the balloon has slipped up and away.

THE CONTRACT

I've wished for peace over and over again, and I've sought it in both expected and unexpected places. My friend Kelly, who'd connected me with Kathryn, the emotional alchemist, also recommended an intuitive therapist she'd been seeing—a traditionally trained therapist who also has intuitive abilities. I reached out to Caroline, because why not? Because despite it all, I had more questions than answers, and I had drenched myself in the asking. I was soaked through with it.

Caroline FaceTimed me, and I answered the call on my laptop. During our first session she talked about the contracts we have with others. In every relationship, she said, there are the things that connect us—things we have in common, things we like about each other. But the contract is like a secret handshake under the table. It's subconscious. It often has to do with the wounds we carry with us from childhood, our attachments, our traumas, even the ones we haven't articulated to ourselves.

I scribbled all of this down on a legal pad in my lap, as fast as I could. I won't say here what she said my contract was—*is*—with my children's father, because I don't think it matters. No, that's not it. I won't say what it is here because it hurts me to think about it.

"For the contract to be broken, finished, both parties have to heal their wounds," she said.

"Wait, so I'm stuck until I heal *and* he does, too?" I didn't want to need him for that.

"You're whole and strong," she said. "You have very clear boundaries. You've outgrown the contract. You're done with it. But now you have to weather him coming to that, too. It could take years."

Years? *Years?!* I told her about ruminating. I told her I couldn't sleep. I could throw everything at my brain—time-release melatonin, magnesium, a drink, a hot bath, lavender oil—and it would still find a way to snap awake at 3:00 in the morning.

"You've got a ghost that follows you around all day," she said.

I know what you're thinking, but no—the ghost wasn't him, it was *me*. She said I was being haunted by the part of me who couldn't set this down. I thought of the don.

Caroline said what I was doing was like tugging on a rope: I pulled, and there was tension on the other side. The only way to stop the tug-of-war was to let go of the rope.

I needed to put the rope down.

A FRIEND SAYS EVERY
BOOK BEGINS WITH AN
UNANSWERABLE QUESTION

Then what is mine?
how to change

SOME PEOPLE ASK

"Do you think you'll get married again?"

People ask this—well-meaning people, people who want me to be settled and happy—and I'm not sure how to answer.

—I could say I've promised my children no changes. That one night, tucking Violet in, lying in bed in the dark beside her, I promised her that no one is moving in, and no one is moving out. I promised her no big family shifts, not anytime soon—no weddings, no stepsiblings, no new babies. I could say that what the kids need now is stability and consistency. They've had no power in how their lives are being shaped. They've watched and waited. They've been told where they will live and when and with whom. I understand, because I only have so much power myself. So I decided to be as constant as I can. I decided to bore the hell out of them with my same-old-same-old love. I could say that yes, it's sometimes lonely doing it on my own. But feeling lonely when you're with your partner is worse than being alone. Being with someone who doesn't want the best for you is worse than being alone. I could say that when I think about my dream partner, what I want in that person is so basic, so low-bar, I'm almost ashamed to say it out loud: Someone who's happy to see me. Someone who smiles when I walk into a room. Someone who can be happy with me and for me—

"I don't know. It's possible. If life has taught me anything, it's that anything's possible." Next question.

PUNCHING BAG

"I have *years* to go," I told my therapist. "Years until my youngest graduates from high school. Years of being legally obligated to maintain contact of some kind with him, before I can just be done."

"Yeah," Megan agreed, "so how can you protect yourself in the meantime? How can you manage it?"

"I don't know. I thought it would be better and easier by now. That's what everyone said in the beginning—don't worry, it'll get easier. It's not easier."

"Well, you can't control anyone else's behavior, so what can you do to manage your expectations?"

I knew what she was getting at, because she'd said it before: *The best predictor for future behavior is past behavior.*

"It's just . . . he still takes up a lot of space in my life for being gone. He was my primary positive relationship at one time, and now it feels like he's my primary *negative* relationship."

I was thinking out loud with her: "Maybe *relationship* is the wrong word. Doesn't a relationship require some reciprocity? Some shared benefit?" I wanted to know what to call it, as if having a name for it would make it make sense. As if naming it would make it manageable.

"It's not like a business partnership," I said. "You wouldn't treat a business partner like this, or you wouldn't be in business."

She was quiet. Waiting. She could see me working it out for myself.

"Take a boxer and a punching bag. The boxer uses the punching bag to get stronger. But what does the punching bag get besides punched?"

She nodded.

"The boxer doesn't have a *relationship* with the punching bag," I said. I realized it as I said it: "We don't have a relationship."

She nodded. "So how do you stop being the punching bag?"

ONE SMALL STEP

I try to follow my therapist's advice. *Boundaries*, she says. *Boundaries, boundaries, boundaries.* I set up a new email account and sent it to my children's father, then blocked him from my personal email. I can only access the new account from my laptop, not my phone, so I don't get any messages from him late at night or first thing in the morning, when I'm in bed. I have enough trouble sleeping as it is. When I check that dedicated email account, I'm at least somewhat prepared for whatever I might find there. Still, each time I click the icon and wait for the inbox to load, I feel a little spike of anxiety. In emails and texts, I do my best to be businesslike, unemotional, detached. There's a term for this, and I'm not using it here.

BIRDS

The week after my kids started back to school full-time, my friend Jessica, an avid birder, came over to visit. Because of the pandemic, we weren't socializing indoors with people outside of our immediate families, so despite the cold we planned to hang out in my backyard.

She brought pizza and little to-go bottles of sangria from one of our favorite restaurants. We sat outside in the cold March wind, bundled up in Adirondack chairs spaced six feet apart, and ate our pizza on paper plates in our laps. We talked about our divorces, our kids, the ways our lives had changed. She said she remembered my baby shower for Violet. We went through births together, miscarriages together, more births together, leaving publishing to go freelance together, and now the ends of our marriages.

What saved her during the worst of her divorce? Birding. It's so engrossing and requires so much focus, you don't think about your kaput marriage or your ex-husband or your legal bills.

"At the end of a day of birding, I realized I hadn't thought about it once," she said.

But my job has been writing—thinking—about it. Stewing in my own juices has been good for me in some ways, and not so good in others. I needed a positive distraction, so she said she'd take me birding sometime. "There are so many birds in your poems!" she said. It's true. Once, during a Q&A, someone raised their hand to ask, "What's with all the birds?" My answer, which was only part of the whole, was this: Birds are wild creatures we have access to no matter where we live. If you're in a city or a suburb, you get the wilderness of birds. I was reminded of driving down High Street past a Giant Eagle grocery store with Rhett in the backseat. He looked over and saw the bird's nests in some of the letters on the sign. *G, A, E.* "What letters in your name would be best for a bird's nest?" he asked. I loved—*love*—his mind.

Balancing a plate of pizza in my lap, I said to Jessica, "My life is unrecognizable from what it was five years ago."

Then we were both quiet, and I reconsidered. I took it back. No, it was about constants and variables. When I looked again, I saw that everything important was the same: I was mothering my two children in my house. They were in the same schools with the same teachers. My neighbors were the same, my friends and family were the same. My office looked out on the same street. The same dogs walked by daily, and I greeted them by name—Molly, Brutus, Lily, Monkey. I recognized my life.

The thing about birds: If we knew nothing of jays or wrens or sparrows, we'd believe the trees were singing, as if each tree has its own song.

The thing about this life: If we knew nothing of what was missing, what has been removed, it would look full and beautiful.

BEES

This is a story about magical thinking, but magical thinking only gets you so far.

One Sunday on Memorial Day weekend, when Violet was only two, I walked into my backyard to take the trash out to the alley behind our house. I stopped when I heard the droning. I heard it before I saw it: a tornado of bees. I remember the feverish vibrato as they spun a column of themselves about my size. I slowly backed up and took the trash back into the house.

We called exterminators, pest control companies, wildlife rescue—anyone we could think of to solve the problem. But it was a holiday weekend, and besides, if they were honeybees—I didn't get close enough to see—they're protected.

It was spring in the suburbs, and we'd ordered three items to be delivered to the house later that afternoon: a grill, a swing set to be assembled, a lawn mower. We took Violet to splash in the fountains at Capital University, trying to keep her away from the bees.

Later, the Lowe's truck arrived, and the man climbed out with his clipboard. By that time, the bees had gathered into what looked like a boiling beach ball in one of the honey locust tree's bad elbows. I explained to the driver: "We've got a bee problem in the backyard, so please just leave everything on the side of the house so you don't get too close. I don't want anyone to get stung."

And what he said next is something that, when I think of it now, makes me wonder about magic.

"I'm a beekeeper."

He worked part-time for Lowe's, but he and his nephew kept bees on their farm not too far outside Columbus.

"We need a new queen," he said, "so if you can wait, we can come back later after my shift and take them for you."

Sure enough, the beekeeper and his nephew came back to our house with their bee boxes and suits, and they smoked the bees out of our tree with lit cigarettes. I kid you not.

When they left, there was only a vibrating fist of bees left in the tree—the workers too dim to leave, the ones who never got the message that the queen was in the box. For days they buzzed away in ones and twos.

What are the odds of walking into a tornado of bees in your backyard on the same day a beekeeper, working part-time driving a delivery truck, arrives?

This is a story about magical thinking. About coincidence and manifestation.

Years later, my children's father called them to tell them some news: The Addressee looked into their backyard and saw a swarm of bees. But the bees didn't gather into a tree's elbow, and a beekeeper didn't serendipitously arrive to take them away. No, the bees funneled into a hole in the side of their house, and they had to have a professional come and extract them. Almost fifty thousand bees were living in the side of their house, he told the kids, and sent them pictures of honeycomb pulled from the walls.

Washing dishes in the kitchen, I caught snippets of the phone call on speakerphone in the other room. I wonder if they heard me reflexively cackle when I heard the words *fifty thousand bees*.

I texted my friend Kelly: *fifty thousand bees to extract, plus honeycomb*.

You know that shit is karma, she texted back.

How many times have I almost slipped and called him *honey*, out of habit? But there's no more sweetness. Two stories, two houses, two tornados of bees. In the first story, a beekeeper arrives, unbidden. In the other, the swarm fills the walls.

WHEN THE METAPHOR IS RIGHT THERE

Rhett has always been an early riser, so on weekends, the day's soft opening is often a "nature show," as we call them. He comes quietly into my dark bedroom to wake me, often curling up beside me to tell me his dreams, and we head downstairs together. He chooses a nature documentary, I make him a simple breakfast, and he begins the show while I make my coffee. Then we curl up side by side, the dog sandwiched between us, and we drink up all the new facts about hummingbirds, beavers, trees, skunks, dogs, crows, the Amazon rainforest, dancing birds, coral. And yes, sometimes bees.

In one, hyena cubs are raised in a pack by only the mothers. "The males," the narrator tells us, "do not play an active role in parenting."

In another, a grasshopper mouse eats a scorpion. The mouse is stung again and again, but his body quiets the pain. After the last translucent, crunchy bite, he stands on his hind legs in the desert moonlight and howls. The tiny mouse howls like a wolf.

In another, the missing rivers of the Yucatán flow underground, through caves. They flow under chandeliers of salt and stone.

In another, we learn that parrots live eighty years. They form a mate bond with their owner. One couple, a man and woman, adopt a parrot as a baby, and he bonds with the man. When the man goes away on business for a week, then returns late at night, going straight to bed without spending time with the bird, they wake to find the parrot had picked all of the feathers from his chest. The parrot had missed the man that much—enough to self-harm, self-mutilate, his whole torso bald and enflamed. I cringe. I have to look away.

In another, we learn that coral and jellyfish are technically immortal. If in a safe environment, they would live forever.

ABOVE THE REAL

Before the new school year started, I had to update the children's information online: address, medical information, emergency contacts.

I input their father's home address and checked the box for "receive mail" but not for "emergency contact." The emergency contacts for the kids are myself and my mother. Because we're here. It's not a metaphor, not a symbol, it just is.

Surreal doesn't mean "unreal." The root, *sur*, means "over" or "above." *Surreal* means "more than real," or "above the real." Too much.

Years ago, when we were twenty-eight, my children's father and I spoke vows—promises—in front of the people we loved most at the time. Our children, the people I love most now, were not in the room. We don't speak vows to our children when they're born. There's no formal process by which we tether ourselves to them. The vows are unspoken, but they hover in the air around us, moving around and in and through everything we say and do. *I will always be here for you. I will protect you. I will make sacrifices for you. I am yours, always.* There is no box on the form to check for that.

How I picture it: For years we lived inside a sort of snow globe, protected. Something had crystallized, gemlike, around us.

I believed we could withstand the snow globe being lifted, shaken, and set back down again. I believed we would withstand it. Things would change, but we would still be us.

It's as if I had lived under a spell, dazed by the falling snow and how it sparkled, unaware of the reality of my own life. But I did not call it a spell until it had been broken.

I did not call it a spell—I called it marriage, family, life.

OUTRAGE

After the divorce, Rhett was often anxious at bedtime. He worried that something bad was happening to his father, just across town. He said he worried about me, too, when he slept there. Wherever he was, he thought the other parent might be in danger. But when his father moved out of state, he said he stopped thinking about it. Why? Because his father lived so far away that even if he needed help, there was nothing Rhett could do.

My first thought: The reverse is also true.

My second thought: How strange that utter helplessness would be a kind of comfort. It didn't comfort me, how far away their other parent lived. It didn't help me sleep at night. It made me—*makes* me—deeply sad for my kids. Sad and angry. I think *outraged* is the word, and when I think about how that word sounds, it's as if you raged right out of yourself. There are so many words, and all of them are accurate, and none of them are. *Unfathomable. Unconscionable. Impossible.*

I thought about what I read about the don—"that which possesses me." When my children's father moved away, I raged right out of myself and into the don. I raged right out of myself, and I needed to crawl back inside. I needed to find *mine*. To be back inside myself, at peace.

THE MATERIAL

Reader, I wanted to hand you something you could use. This story is something I carry, but somewhere inside me, I believe this: If this story is at all useful, it'll carry itself.

THIS IS WHAT WE CALL A FULL-CIRCLE MOMENT

My marriage counselor emailed me three years after our last session. She's retired now, but she wanted me to know that she's been giving *Keep Moving* to family members and recommending it to people.

She knows more about my marriage than I share in that book.

She knows what you know now, and then some.

CAREGIVER

"How much is *caregiver* part of your identity? In what ways might you be keeping others down in order to stay up?" Caroline, the intuitive therapist, wasn't letting me off the hook. "Do you need to remain the parent, even in adult relationships?"

I was quiet—I had to sit with that, chew on it, metabolize it—but she filled the silence. "Think about what caregiving requires—people who *need* you. Even if you're not trying to dominate, caregiving is a kind of dominance. Have you surrounded yourself with people who are more submissive? Needier?"

Had I done that? Had I also "parented" adults in my life? My husband? Men I'd dated? Friends? I'd joked for years about having strong firstborn energy—once a bossy big sister, always a bossy big sister—but this wasn't funny.

Then she asked, "What would happen if you dialed your caregiving back from eighty percent to fifty percent? What if you came to your next relationship boundaried and whole?"

Megan, my "regular" therapist, and Caroline, the intuitive therapist, had something in common: They talked a lot about boundaries. I was beginning to think I had a problem setting them. If taking care of others is part of my identity, the story I tell myself about myself, what would happen if I weren't needed as a caregiver? What would the story be?

FORTY THINGS

I called my mother, as I do almost every day, and as soon as she picked up, I handed her some of what I'd been carrying. I was worried that with the move, the kids would see their father as someone whose emotional needs were more pressing than theirs. I was worried they'd feel guilty about their pain and anger, because don't they want him to be happy? Don't they want the best for him? I was worried they wouldn't remember the loving family we once were.

"That's bullshit," she said. I knew she'd probably go out to the garage to light a cigarette. It's her not-so-secret secret habit.

"He was so loved, not just by you but by all of us. He had a whole family of people who loved him, really loved him—me, your dad, your sisters, their husbands, the grandparents and aunts and uncles. He had all of us. All of us."

"I know, Mom," I said quietly. I did know.

"When you guys used to come over here for Sunday dinner, you'd just curl up on the couch together, snuggling, telling little inside jokes. It used to piss me off, because you never offered to help with anything. You were in your own world. Even after Violet you were like that."

"I don't remember that," I said, because I didn't.

"Do you remember what he did for you on your fortieth birthday? He made a list of forty things he loved about you. Handwritten. You sent a picture of it to me."

"He did? I don't remember that. I don't know what happened to it."

When I drove to my parents' house one afternoon in late summer and told my mother, finally, that my marriage was in trouble, I said, "I think he's leaving."

And she just said, "Who? Leaving to go where?" She couldn't imagine what I would say next. Later she'd tell me on the phone that we were the last couple she would have expected to divorce. That we seemed meant to be together, perfect for each other.

Apparently, we were not.

I put the call on speaker, put the phone on my bed, and found the box where I keep many of my most precious things. I figured the fortieth-birthday list might be in there, but it wasn't. There were letters and cards from him, but I didn't find the list. I didn't know where it was or what was on it. What were those forty things?

"I have no idea what happened to it, Mom."

POSTCARD

I can still see the first sentence in his unmistakable handwriting. It's not for your eyes, and of course it was not meant for mine. I still have questions about what he'd written her. Had he promised her a letter but was sending a postcard instead? Or had he been writing her letters, and the postcard—brief, less intimate—was a change? Many of the letters he wrote me over the years are still in that box of precious things, most of them on yellow legal paper, folded neatly in thirds. I don't look at them, searching for answers or clues. I can't imagine the children will want them. Why am I keeping those letters?

THE THINGS

I don't know what to do with the things—the stuff of a marriage, a life. All the things we registered for when we decided to get married—the dishes and silverware, the barware, the serving platters, the bath towels, the picture frames. And what to do with the pictures inside them—the wedding pictures and family pictures and candid shots. In some, because all of the babies were on the floor in their bouncy seats and on their play mats or in their exersaucers (what is the hybrid there? *exercise? sauce? exertion?*), sometimes their father's shoes or blue-jeaned calves are in the photos. Or I can see a mug I know is his, or a piece of furniture or art he took when he left, and it ruins the whole damn photo for me. I understand now why people physically cut up wedding photos and family photos. Because you want to preserve the part you love and remove—excise, surgically—the part you don't. Or, rather, the part that hurts you.

There are pieces of him hidden like little landmines everywhere: his handwriting in our cookbooks, tweaking recipes to his taste; the framed selfie of him in Rhett's bedroom; the mail that comes for him to our house each week; the postcards he occasionally sends to the children; even our children—their hyphenated last names, and their faces in certain light, at certain times of day.

I replaced what I had to when he moved out, and I've continued to replace what I can afford to, bit by bit: new bed, new mattress, new dining table and chairs, new dining cabinets, new bookshelves, new coffee tables, new art on the walls. When I finally bought a new couch, a yellow midcentury modern sectional, Violet complained, "But the old couch is tradition. You're replacing everything."

I didn't say: *The only way I can live in this house is if it's my house. Our house. The only way I can remain is if I change it.*

But I haven't changed everything. I still eat off the wedding registry dishes, almost all of them chipped now, with the wedding registry silverware. I still drink from the highball glasses and champagne flutes we received as wedding gifts. When I step out of the shower, I wrap myself in one of our old bath towels, now all bleached out and unraveling.

My wedding dress is still hanging in Rhett's bedroom closet. My rings are in a porcelain, heart-shaped dish on my dresser—the one I hid tiny, lucky things inside when I was a child. I remember early on wanting to sell or pawn my diamond engagement ring, and taking whatever money I could get and using it on a writing retreat or a fun road trip with the kids. I also considered just throwing it off a bridge. I haven't done either of those things, but I still might do either one.

How I picture it: We are nesting dolls, carrying all of our earlier selves inside us. I feel so full of the life I had before—the life I have already lived—how is there room for anything new?

We feel and feel, and live and live, but somehow we're never full. This life is elastic, impossibly elastic. There is always room for more experience. Our lives expand to accommodate anything.

GREAT WHITE

In the first few months after the children's father moved out of state, I talked to my therapist twice a month. Each session began with a recap of what had happened since we last spoke, and between litigation and the kids and work, it was always a lot. *A lot* a lot.

But I remember one time we spoke, it had been a quiet week—no infuriating emails or texts, no demands from the lawyers, nothing that left me feeling triggered.

"That's good, right?" Megan asked.

I told her: It's like *Jaws*. When the shark is gnawing at the boat, of course it's terrifying—the only thing you can focus on is those teeth and staying the hell away from them. But when the dorsal fin disappears underwater, it's not over. It's not safe, and you don't get to relax. The shark isn't gone, it's just trying to find another way into the boat.

(*Great white*, it occurred to me later. *Great white*. That's what our wedding dishes are called.)

Litigation can feel like terrorism—domestic litigation especially, because it's personal, not close to home but *in* your home—and I think that's by design. People who are upset, exhausted, and hemorrhaging money might be willing to concede things they otherwise wouldn't concede. Just to make it stop. Just to keep the boat afloat.

I told my therapist that what I want more than anything is to be free. To parent my children, do my work, and serenity prayer the rest. I use *serenity prayer* as a verb the way I use *eternal sunshine* as a verb, as in, "I'm trying to serenity prayer the shit out of this time of my life." As in, "I wish I could eternal sunshine most of this time right out of my mind."

I have become an exile from my own history.

—Rachel Cusk

THE INTANGIBLES

"You know what one of the saddest damn things is? One of the parts of all this that I'm grieving the most? When I lost my marriage, I lost all that shared history. I lost the person who knew me in a way no one else does, and when I lost him, I also lost being known like that."

Megan, my therapist, looked at me through the screen. She nodded but didn't speak. She knew me well enough to know I was going to keep talking.

"I mean, it's all the little things," I said. "The private jokes and made-up songs and silly voices and comedy bits we'd do."

I didn't tell her that on taco night, we'd sing "taco night" to the tune of the Village People's "Macho Man." I didn't tell her that my husband used to tell me he loved me "mucho mucho," or that he addressed my letters and cards to Martha from George, because one of our favorite films was *Who's Afraid of Virginia Woolf?* The irony of that film being about a dysfunctional marriage would not have been lost on Megan.

"All that shared history, all that institutional knowledge from the marriage—what do I do with it? What do I do when a little piece from my old life floats to the surface and bobs there right in front of my face. Who do I tell? Who do I laugh with or sing along with?"

She nodded. "So, how does it make you feel in the moment, when you remember something like that? How do you handle it?"

"I don't know how I feel. Sad? Swindled? Cheated out of something? There's no joint custody for intangibles. We can't just divide them up like dishes or artwork. There is no selling off memories and splitting the proceeds."

Who is awarded Lyle Lovett's "Nobody Knows Me"? It was our wedding song. I wanted it, but it wasn't mine to keep. Who gets to claim the Cliffs of Moher, or the road winding along Oak Creek between Sedona and the Grand Canyon, or the frantic run to catch the train in Paris? I didn't ask her, because I knew the answer. We both get everything and nothing at all, and that, I tell her, is the saddest damn thing.

JOKE*

Have you heard the one about the middle-aged woman who can't make her own tears? The one about the woman with chronic dry eye who can (sort of) afford her health insurance premium *or* the prescription eyedrops, but not both? The one about the woman whose husband redlined her tears on the page, and now they're gone—redacted, deleted—from her actual eyes?

Have you heard the one about the sad woman who can't afford her tears? It's hilarious. She could laugh about it until she cries, if only.

---

* I wanted this book to have more levity. More than that, I wanted the *life* to have more levity. Reader, I wish I could offer you 20 percent more wit and 20 percent less pain, and I wish life had offered me those bonuses and discounts, too. But to play devil's advocate: It's okay to have feelings. You don't have to laugh them off. You don't have to turn everything painful that happens into a self-deprecating joke in which you and your suffering are the punchline. It's okay to put away the sad trombone. It's okay to show up as your whole self, to come as you are.

IT WASN'T ALL BAD

One day, seemingly out of the blue, I remembered a conversation I had with my husband when the publisher of my third book wanted to change the title from *Weep Up* to *Good Bones*. I was wedded to the original title—my daughter's words—and bristled at the proposed change. It felt, at times, that this single poem was taking over everything else.

I'd called my husband at work, and I was pacing in the backyard, as I still do when I talk on the phone. He made a good point: I wanted people to read the book, right? Isn't that the point—to have people read my work? And wouldn't more people find the book if the title is this poem they've been reading everywhere? Yes, yes, yes, I agreed, so the title was changed.

I want you to know that it wasn't all bad. We were a family once—first we were two, then three, then four. At one time there were forty things he loved about me. I'm a few years older now, so there would be a few more things. Except there aren't. We've spent the last few years subtracting from that number.

ANOTHER MOTHER'S DAY

Imagine that contentious and expensive litigation is dragging on and on, despite you trying to settle months earlier, saying, *I need to stop the bleeding.* That story isn't one I'll tell here, but know this: It did not have to go on that long, and it did not have to cost, financially or psychologically, what it cost.

Now imagine, in the middle of all this, it's Mother's Day. That morning, my phone dinged: a text from my children's father. He wanted me to know that our two children were wonderful due in no small part to me.

I did not respond, *This is like praising the culture of a country while shelling it relentlessly. "Hey, you sure have beautiful music, delicious food, and loving, open people," he says, dropping bomb after bomb.*

I did not respond, *You are not what you say, you are what you do.*

I did not respond, *This is like punching someone in the face while telling them they're terrific—not even punching them,* then *telling them how wonderful they are, not even like apology flowers from an abusive partner, or a bonus from an asshole boss. No, it's concurrent. The punch and the flowers are happening at the same time.*

I did not respond, *My mother loved you as her own son and you broke her heart.*

I did not respond, *You moved five hundred miles away from those two wonderful kids.*

Nothing exists in a vacuum. A text—like a letter, a poem, or story, a piece of art—exists in a historical, social, and political context. All you have to do is look at when it was created and ask yourself, *What else was happening then?*

What else was happening in our lives then?

Oh.

The punch and the flowers were happening at the same time.

SOME PEOPLE WILL ASK

"What about your children? Don't you want to protect your children?" Someone will ask this, maybe even you.

Is this a question you want me to answer?

None of these answers are secret or even hypothetical. There's nothing I'm holding back here, nothing that will remain unsaid.

I'll say that my children won't read this book for years, if ever. I'll say that the most painful parts of this story aren't secrets to them. They live this story, all of it, even the parts I haven't shared here. I'll say kids always know more than we think they do. I'll say that I don't believe in secrets or lies as "protection" because secrets rust. They make your chest cavity look like the hull of some ship at the bottom of the sea—eaten by salt, corroded. I'll say that I believe in honesty as care. I'll say that I know my children love me, and they love their father, and I hope they forgive us for all the things we are not, because what we are is human.

There are years that question and years that answer.

—Zora Neale Hurston

YEARS THAT QUESTION

The years since my marriage ended have felt like rapid-fire Q&A, light on the A. Reader, we've gotten this far together, in years recounted, in pages turned—shouldn't there be more answers? In any mystery, the answers tend to arrive in disguise. So often they're clothed in trouble. Why do answers wear trouble so well? Maybe because they need to get our attention.

If I don't recognize the answers, they try another way. Plan B, Plan C, Plan D. (As my kids have said, "Mom, as long as we don't get to Plan Z, we're okay.") Sometimes many plans are necessary, a whole alphabet of plans. Sometimes I need to hear the same thing in different words from different people, different sources, before I really hear it. The answer knocks on all the doors, tries all the windows, then slips in over the transom if it must.

One afternoon, scrolling social media, I read a phrase that broke over me like a wave I didn't see coming: *inability to metabolize disappointment.* This is what the writer Elissa Altman saw when looking at an old photograph of her mother: a woman whose life did not turn out the way she'd expected. I thought about Kathryn, the emotional alchemist, who described this as her work—helping people metabolize their experiences. What happens if you don't process what has happened to you, what you've done, what you didn't do? It sits inside you. It can make you feel like you're choking, like you can't take a full breath.

In a divorce, the question is so often "Why?" I may never know for sure, but clues are arriving, knocking on the door, rattling the windows. They prickle along the back of my neck. They're dressed head to toe in trouble, and they always find a way in. Plan E, Plan F, Plan G.

"Wish for more pain," a friend's therapist advised, if you want to change. If you're in enough pain, you won't be able to continue living the way you've been living; you'll have to do something differently. But be careful what you wish for, because you just might get it—and then what? Then the pain is yours. The pain is yours and it will change you.

THE PLAY

The curtain hasn't fallen. The play continues, but The Finder still has no script. The longer the run, the better she gets at improv.

In this scene, she delivers a monologue, speaking from a lit corner of the dark stage. She addresses—who? In the beginning of the play, he was The Husband. He's no longer that. She addresses her children's father, her ex-husband, addresser of postcards. She addresses The Addresser.

Let me tell you what you don't know, what you would know if you were still part of my life. I can cook now, like, really cook. I have more tattoos. I can throw a baseball with the same speed and accuracy with my right and left hands. Our neighbor taught me how to use the lawn mower, and he replaced the carburetor on the trimmer, and he taught me how to use that, too. All the stuff you left behind in the basement is gone. I dragged it to the alley in a rainstorm after you moved away, and whatever passersby didn't claim, the trash collectors took. You broke my mother's heart, my father's heart, my sisters' hearts. I still hear from people I thought were "your people," so I suppose they're my people, too. Sometimes I still wear the perfume I wore on our wedding day, because I like it. I've never felt better. I've never felt worse. Your absence has made the life I have now possible. In which case, thank you. I didn't ask for more pain, but I received it—you sent it—and it changed me. Thank you.

Memory itself is a kind of architecture.
                                    —Louise Bourgeois

. . . form is never more than an extension of content.
                                    —Robert Creeley

THE MATERIAL

The way I'm telling you this story—these pieces, these strands, these echoes—*is* the story. There is no way to divorce form from content.

There was a pinecone, brought home as a souvenir from a business trip, given to my son. I threw the pinecone away, as if it were infected, as if by throwing it away I could protect us from what it symbolized.

All of it is gone now—the pinecone, the postcard, the pages in the notebook. All that material, discarded. But what they symbolize remains. My children's father moved to a real house I've never been inside in a real state I've never visited to live with a real woman I've never met. No symbols here, only facts. This is my material.

THE SCRAPS

Whenever I want to remember how many years my parents have been married, I add four to my age. My mother married at twenty, then had me at twenty-four, my sister Katie at twenty-six, and my sister Carly at twenty-eight. Twenty-eight years old and already married eight years? Twenty-eight years old with three kids under age four? I can't imagine it.

On my parents' forty-eighth wedding anniversary, it struck me: forty-eight years is more than I have left to live. Even if I were to remarry, I would never be married for that long. I don't have enough time. This is something else I mourn. My chance at a golden anniversary, at growing old with someone who knew me when I was young, died in the divorce.

After I was a guest on his podcast, the singer-songwriter Rhett Miller—yes, the Rhett my son is named for—invited me to send along song ideas if I ever had them. Poems and songs aren't the same, but they both rely on voice and form, rhythm and sound play, metaphor and image, repetition and surprise. I wrote to Rhett about "the scraps"—the leftover bits of a life after the "real" life, the "real" relationship, is over. What do we do with the years we have left? How do we begin again in a sort of afterlife? Maybe a week later, he texted me a photo of a typewritten page—a start.

The Scraps

Maybe things get better in the aftermath
Or maybe all you're left with is the scraps
The oddities and endings
The mangled beyond mending
The wondering what comes after that
Maybe all you're left with is the scraps

A NOTE ON FORM

Let me tell you a little about the cento. It's a kind of poem assembled using the lines of other poets. Memory, too, is assemblage—a kind of cento, collaged from pieces. From the scraps of a life.

Writing this book, bit by bit, I felt compelled to assemble a lyric essay using sentences pulled from throughout these pages. I suspected that images might gravitate toward one another, as if magnetized: strings and tethers, a heart and the pit of a fruit, various ghosts and hauntings and disappearances. I suspected that the pieces might speak to each other more clearly if I allowed them to be part of a new whole. So I invited sentences to sidle up next to each other, although they were strangers at first, and whisper in each other's ears like friends. They could be in close, intimate conversation rather than having to call across pages and pages, as if shouting into the wind on either side of a wide canyon.

William James used a term I find myself returning to often: *torn-to-pieces-hood*. This was his translation of the German word *Zerrissenheit*, which carries inside it a sense of tornness, brokenness, disconnection, disjointedness. When I think of the torn-to-pieces-hood, I can't help but think of the "multitudes" Walt Whitman celebrates in himself. Sometimes I'm weary of how torn and pieced and layered those multitudes feel, how fragmented and contradictory in ways that thrill me and scare me, but I want to celebrate them, too. Bringing the pieces together is part of that celebration.

A KIND OF CENTO, COLLAGED FROM PIECES OF THE WHOLE

If I knew so little of the life I called my own, can I still claim it as mine? The answer is yes. The answer knocks on all the doors, tries all the windows, slips in over the transom if it must. No, it wasn't always like this, not exactly. I floated through the house, practically transparent. Is this what living is—trusting the string to hold?

Next question. How can I make this material into a tool you can use? There is a difference between what is built in the body and what is built in the imagination. "Something's wrong, something's wrong with my heart," I said. I can't bear to think of it in there somewhere, like the perfect pit of some otherwise rotten fruit. For a while I carried it inside me like a small, sharp thing that cut me when I moved wrong.

I've become a student of my own pain, my own grief and suffering. In this way, he has been my teacher? Everything we learn, we learn from someone who is imperfect. We all come into the world less than done, unfinished, our skulls still stitching themselves together. All wax and feathers, a mess of hope.

This is a story about magical thinking. Then he's unwriting it, his handwriting disappearing letter by letter from the blank side. Times does these things, too.

We both get everything and nothing at all. Two houses, two beds, two Christmases, two birthdays. And yet, there is foreshadowing everywhere, foreshadowing I would have seen myself if I'd been reading a novel or watching a film, not living a life.

The house was full of hidden valentines. It was—*is*—my life. I live in the heart of the heart of it all. I'm the same, I'm just me, I'm right here.

How I picture it: I am not a half-double now. I am not half of anything. What I am is singular. Whole.

A NOTE ON THE TITLE

When I first started writing this book, I joked that a more accurate title might be *Notes from a Shipwreck* or *Anecdotes from an Airship in Flames*. Because, well, truth in advertising.

But the more time passed, the less I hurt. The less I hurt, the more I was able to see how beautiful, how full, my life was. I felt myself smiling as I walked in my neighborhood. My eyes followed the calls of birds to find them in the trees—grackles, woodpeckers, crows, robins, blue jays, cardinals. I'd built a life in which my days were like this: taking long walks, writing, mothering, cackling over coffee or cocktails with friends, sleeping alone some nights, being held close by someone I loved other nights. I was unfolding, learning to take up space. Life began to feel open enough, elastic enough, to contain whatever I might choose for it.

Now I see the title as a call to action—a promise I'd made not only to this book, and to you, but to myself. A promise I intend to keep.

MAGICAL THINKING

It was Easter and I'd fucked up. I had the kids that Sunday, but their father was here visiting for a couple of days before. Would the Easter Bunny visit their Airbnb? Would they have an egg hunt with him, baskets of candy, the whole shebang? I had no idea.

Rhett asked if the Easter Bunny was coming to our house, and I froze. I must have had a strange look on my face, because then he said, "Okay, okay, what's going on? Is the Easter Bunny real? You can tell me the truth."

I looked at Violet sheepishly, then she and I both started laughing. "Okay, fine. No, the Easter Bunny isn't real."

Rhett's eyes got wide, but he cracked a smile. "You?! You've been doing this the whole time? The eggs and the candy, and . . . everything?"

"Yes, honey. It's been me all along."

His sister stood beside him, projecting wisdom. She'd known this for a few years already.

"Well, that's kind of a bummer," he said. "But also—thanks! That's a lot of work!"

That was that. There was no Easter Bunny, but everything else was still real to him—Santa and his elves, the Tooth Fairy, garden fairies, leprechauns. I knew it, though: Now that one card had been pulled, it wouldn't be long before the whole house came down.

A few weeks later, Rhett asked me about the Tooth Fairy. "Honey, we've already been over this," I said. "You know the Tooth Fairy isn't real."

"What?!" He was genuinely shocked.

I'd fucked up again. I'd confused the Easter Bunny talk, which had happened, with the Tooth Fairy talk, which most certainly had *not* happened. But it was too late.

"*You've* been taking my teeth and leaving me money?! What do you do with them?"

We went upstairs, where Violet had heard the commotion.

"Mom's the Tooth Fairy!" he said to her, incredulously.

"Dude, I know," she said, with teenage flatness.

They followed me into my bedroom. I opened my top dresser drawer and dug in the back for an earring box. I shook it, heard its delicate rattle, and knew it was the right one. I removed the lid and held the box out to them, so they could see all the tiny, sharp baby teeth, like bits of broken seashell. Some of them still had dark dried blood inside them.

"These are mostly Violet's," I said. "But they're probably all mixed together at this point."

They agreed: It was gross, and frankly like something out of a horror movie, and I should put the box away.

One more card in the house, pulled. I knew Santa would be next. So many spells have been broken since the divorce, I wondered how long I could preserve the last of the magic.

A NOTE ON PLOT

Even as the story continues, this book will end. I know this. I'm running out of time and space, running out of pages, to answer these unanswerable questions. I'm trying on so many metaphors, pushing toward understanding. I'm trying on so many lines written by others but through which I can see my own experience.

I've wanted for years to understand what happened, and part of me feels I've failed because I don't fully understand—*can't* fully understand because I don't have access to the whole picture. I only have access to the *mine*.

What now? *I am out with lanterns, looking for myself.* But here's the thing about carrying light with you: No matter where you go, and no matter what you find—or *don't* find—you change the darkness just by entering it. You clear a path through it.

This flickering? It's mine. This path is mine.

A FRIEND SAYS EVERY BOOK BEGINS WITH AN UNANSWERABLE QUESTION

Then what is mine?
how to make this place beautiful

GOLDEN

After my parents' forty-eighth wedding anniversary, I thought more about long-term commitment and devotion. I thought more about the unspoken vows we make to the people we love, and how those promises hover in the air around us, touching everything we say and do. I thought more about the time I have left and the relationships I have or am yet to have. I thought more about "the scraps."

Then something else struck me: When I turn forty-eight, I will have forty-eight years in a loving relationship with my parents. When my sisters each turn forty-eight, I will have forty-eight years with them. When my children each turn forty-eight, I will have forty-eight years of being their mother. That's as golden as it gets.

RAINBOW CONNECTION

Sometimes being a parent feels like being in a country where you don't speak the language. Violet's tales from middle school are peppered with words like *mid*, *sus*, *vibey*, and *aesthetic*. When she tried to define *emo* for me, it was like a scene from an indie movie: exasperated teenager, out-of-touch mom. Even now, I remember being on the *other* side of that dynamic with my own mother.

Still, while we aren't always using the same vocabulary, Violet and I talk—a lot. We're close, and we're similar in many ways, both introverted, creative, curious, and sarcastic. But the one thing we connect over more than anything else? Our love of music.

I've been sharing music with both of my kids since before they were even born; it's part of how I show love. The mix CD I made to take to the hospital for Violet's birth—the one with *Welcome, Pickle!* written on the mirrored disc in Sharpie—including Ray LaMontagne's "You Are the Best Thing," Band of Horses' "No One's Gonna Love You," and Wilco's "My Darling." Rhett's playlist included John Lennon's "Beautiful Boy," The The's "This Is the Day," and the Innocence Mission's cover of "What a Wonderful World."

As my children grew, I put a CD case in our hallway, marked "Little Free Music Library," where they could borrow my CDs. Some they took to immediately—Bowie, Prince, Queen—but not all. Violet still hasn't warmed up to Andrew Bird; something about the whistling gets under her skin. Rhett wasn't a fan of the Beastie Boys at first: "Mom, I know this does it for you, but it doesn't really do it for me." But one road trip with *Paul's Boutique* turned up loud in the car later, he's a convert.

Sharing music with them came naturally, since that's one of the ways I've bonded with my own parents. When I turned on the radio in middle school, I'd hear Wilson Phillips or Poison, but my walls were covered in Beatles posters. I have my mom and dad to thank for that. We'd put on a record from their extensive collection—mostly '70s rock and folk, '80s pop, Motown—and sing along while my mom cooked or we did housework. My dad took me to National Record Mart to buy my first tape. He couldn't decide whether *Rubber Soul* or *Revolver* was the more seminal album, so I came home with both.

The soundtrack of my childhood was my parents' record collection: Elton John, Dan Fogelberg, the Bee Gees, Marvin Gaye, Donna Summer, America, and yes, The Beatles. Early in the pandemic, my dad packed up the whole collection in plastic crates and gave it to me, so now I have all the albums we listened to when I was a kid—not just the songs, but the actual, physical records our hands touched back then. Some of them are too scratched to play anymore, but others we listen to while I cook or we do housework.

Violet, already well beyond my old CD library, is becoming a master playlist maker. She draws or collages in her room (her lair, as I call it), listening to music on her phone, gathering songs the way a magpie gathers shiny things. Violet has playlists for different vibes (cue my daughter rolling her eyes at me for using that word here), different times of year, different people, and her love shines through in those playlists.

She made one of her brother's favorite songs: "Seat 16B" by Hello Emerson, "Chinatown" by Luna, "Scared of the Dark" by Lil Wayne, from the *Spider-Man: Into the Spiderverse* soundtrack. It touched me to see "Rhett loves these songs" pop up in her list of playlists.

Recently, she gave *me* a gift I've treasured every day since: a playlist she made called "Hey Mom." It began as four hours and fifty-seven minutes of my favorite songs or songs that mean something to the two of us, and she's continually adding to it. It's now over seven hours long. I play it on shuffle when I walk the dog or run errands in the car, always happy to hear Superchunk, The Replacements, Fruit Bats, Metric, and Teenage Fanclub—songs I love, yes, but more importantly, songs she *noticed* I love. It's the audio equivalent of a hug from my daughter.

Reader, I must confess: I was afraid to have a teenage daughter. I was afraid to have a teenage girl in my house because I *was* a teenage girl, and I was mouthy, rebellious, and sneaky. There was plenty of eye-rolling, back talking, and door slamming. Since Violet was young, maybe seven or eight years old, we've been talking about the teenage years and what can happen between mothers and daughters. *I just want you to keep talking to me,* I told her. *If you think I'm being too strict, or if I think you're pushing things too far, let's just talk.* I tell her the same thing now: *Let's always keep the lines of communication open, no matter what.*

Here's the thing about my teenage daughter: I love her, but I also like her. A lot.

The last time we watched *The Muppet Movie,* the kids and I snuggled up together with the dog on the couch, of course I teared up when Kermit sang "Rainbow Connection," as I always do. The opening banjo music gets me every single time. A few days later, when we were all in the car together, I cued up the "Hey Mom" playlist on shuffle. "Rainbow Connection" started up. I looked over at Violet in the passenger seat, and she smiled back at me. "I just added it," she said.

I swallowed the lump in my throat, and we all sang along.

IT GETS PRETTY WOO HERE

"They chose you. They chose you both, and they knew what the challenges would be." Caroline, the intuitive therapist, was talking to me through my laptop screen, and she was talking about my children.

It had never occurred to me before that children might choose their parents, but this is what she believes. And she believes that when we choose our parents, we know their limitations. We know the ways we will be hurt by them, or let down by them, and we choose them anyway. She believes the lessons we need to learn in this lifetime are tied to the parents we choose.

I don't know if I can believe that I chose my parents, but I know this: I'd choose them now, again and again.

I don't know if I can believe that my children chose me, that they chose to come to this earth through me, but what a privilege to think that they saw me as worthy. That they saw us, as a pair, as worthy. We hit the jackpot.

If indeed they did, I want to ask them: Am I the mother you wanted? The one you expected? Has none of this life been a surprise to you?

It's been a surprise to me. There are so many beautiful and terrible things I didn't see coming, so much dark water under the boat, so much land still unexplored. If indeed they chose me, I want to tell them: Thank you. Most of all: Thank you.

UPDATING AND UNBLURRING

The last photo of my house on Google Maps is dated October 2019. That month, on what would have been our fourteenth wedding anniversary, I refinanced the house so that it is in my name only now. It's mine. No, it's *ours*—the kids' and mine.

Worrying about the house was the part of the divorce I felt most in my body: the trying desperately to stay, to keep my kids in the only home they'd ever known. Many nights I'd wake up, heart racing, sweating from the stress of it. How could a self-employed writer buy a litigator out of a house? What would I have to negotiate away? The answer: plenty. But I did it. I didn't think I could do it, and I did it.

On my former wedding anniversary, a kind woman from the title company came to my home, and we sat down together at the dining room table, where I signed the tall stack of paperwork. Later I dropped a cashier's check for my ex-husband's portion of the equity into the mail slot at his rental house nearby—he still lived nearby then—and I drove home.

In the October 2019 photo of my house—*my* house—on Google Maps, I see two small pumpkins on the porch. In the front yard, among fallen leaves, political signs I can't read, their text blurred. Inside, there were no men's shoes under the dining room table, no stained teacups. The children may have been home, or at school, or at their father's house that day. My car is the only one in the driveway.

When I see the next photo, whenever it is taken, I'll know Rhett's room is upstairs, painted yellow by his mother and father, with some help by a three-year-old Violet wearing an old tee shirt of mine as a smock. I'll know my room is right next to his, and Violet's room is right across the hall, primed and painted with love by my father.

I'll see my home. Our home.

FULL DISCLOSURE

Keep Moving kept us in this house. Or rather, the advance for the book I wrote about enduring my divorce kept me from losing our home in the divorce. I have to chew on that some more. I have to metabolize that: My work was not the problem. My work was the solution. I kept us here with words.

I have woven
a parachute out of everything broken . . .
                                        —William Stafford

SOME PEOPLE WILL ASK

"You say you want to forgive. Have you?"

Someone will ask that, I'm sure, because I ask myself all the time. How do I answer?

—I could say it's difficult to forgive someone who hasn't expressed remorse. I could counter with questions: Why do I need to forgive someone who doesn't seem to be sorry? What if forgiveness doesn't need to be the goal? The goal is the wish: peace. Can there be peace without forgiveness? How do you heal when there is an open wound that is being kept open, a scab always being picked until it bleeds again? I could say this is my task: seeking peace, knowing the wound may never fully close—

"Forgiveness is complicated. To be at peace, I think what I need is acceptance. I accept it."

MAGICAL THINKING

On the morning Rhett went around the block on his bike for the first time on his own, I waited for him on the front porch in the sunshine. So what if the neighbors saw my terrible bedhead? When he came back around, I heard him approaching, the sound of bike tires on pavement, and before he even saw me, he began a long "Heeeeeeeeeey," anticipating streaming by me. He turned around in our neighbor's driveway, then pulled up in front of our house.

"How'd it go, buddy?" I asked.

"It makes me feel independent," he said, which made me laugh. I could see it in his posture, his smile, the way he held his chin up slightly.

I was sitting on the top step of the front porch with my coffee, thumbing notes for a poem into my phone, watching him stream by again and again. Like watching the sun rise and set—it doesn't go up and down, it goes around. It comes back. It always comes back.

Sun, son. The homophone isn't lost on me.

I often write down what my children say—the sweet, funny things, or the things that seem impossibly wise or apt. This is one entry from when Rhett was just learning to talk:

Looking out the back door in the morning as the sun rises.
Rhett: Snowy!
Me: And sunny!
Rhett: No sunshine.
Me: What is shining on Mommy's face?
Rhett: Rhett.

After he circled the block a few more times, we sat on the front porch steps together. Fluffy seeds floated in the air around us, and I caught one. I opened my hand. He saw it and said, "Make a wish."

I wished for what I always wish: peace. Whenever I make a wish—birthday candle, eyelash, 11:11, dandelion fluff—I wish for the same thing. To feel at peace is to be free. But this time I rephrased it, to clarify, to make sure the receiver of wishes heard me clearly: *Peace*, I thought. *Resolution*. Resolution—that long, flat stretch in the narrative arc after the crisis. I had lost my narrative, but I wanted to find resolution.

I blew the seed from my hand and it drifted a bit, then settled to the pavement of the front walk.

"It'll come true now, because no one else will wish on it," Rhett said.

"You think if someone makes a wish, and then the fluff reaches someone else, and they make a wish, too, the first wish doesn't come true?"

"Yeah," he said. "Just the second one comes true."

"Well, why wouldn't the first wish call dibs on the fluff, so that if anyone else tried to make a wish on it, it would be full? It couldn't take?"

"Nope. That's not how it works," he said, smiling. He was messing with me.

I don't know how it works. *If* it works. I've been wishing for peace for three years, and no peace. Before peace I wished for my marriage to be salvaged. I've wished against miscarriages that happened, against deaths that happened. But part of me believes—the part of me that has my tarot cards read, talks to an intuitive therapist, reads my horoscope. The part of me that had a beekeeper arrive at my house on the day a swarm of bees descended upon my backyard.

"If you believe in wishes," I told him, "if you believe they can come true, then you should believe that wishes are infinite."

I believe that.

How I picture it: My life is like the ocean that scientists just discovered—something that's been on maps and atlases, hiding in plain view as part of another whole. This new ocean was always there, always itself, but we are only now recognizing it. This is my life, and it's beautiful.

HOW IT ENDS

S omeone asked me, "How will it end?" Meaning this book.

"I have no idea," I said. "I don't even know how to begin." Translation: *I don't fully understand, and I suspect understanding will always be out of reach.*

I remember something the poet Stanley Plumly said to me about poems: "They begin in the middle and they end in the middle, only later." This story begins in the middle and ends . . . where? How? When will we reach the place on the narrative arc as flat as the Ohio landscape, as constant as the heart of the heart?

Earlier I posed a question I couldn't answer: If there had been no postcard, no notebook, would our marriage have survived? I know the answer now. The answer is a gift that assembling these pieces has handed me. The answer is no.

I keep thinking that this story, this life, could've happened another way. In some parallel universe, maybe it did, but here it happened like this—or, rather, it's *happening* like this. How will it end? I don't know. Every ending is one of many possibilities, one of many unknowns. Every ending is secret until it happens.

It's late but everything comes next.
                    —Naomi Shihab Nye

Then I know that there is room in me
for a second huge and timeless life.
                    —Rainer Maria Rilke, translated by Robert Bly

CALLING MYSELF DARLING

When my poem "Bride" was first published, I was in Florida teaching a weeklong workshop at a poetry festival. Each day, between morning classes and afternoon lectures and panel discussions, I managed to carve out enough free time to walk a little over a mile from my hotel to the beach. As an Ohioan, I couldn't be *that* close to the Atlantic and not gape at it as often as possible. On that day I stopped at the news shop, picked up two copies of the *New Yorker*, and carried them down to the beach in my tote bag. I sat down on a bench, pulled off my boots and socks, then walked barefoot across the sand to the slap and fizz of the waves breaking.

Something about being at the ocean always reminds me of how small I am, but not in a way that makes me feel insignificant. It's a smallness that makes me feel a part of the world, not separate from it. I sat down in a lounge chair and opened the magazine to my poem, the thin pages flapping in the wind. In that moment, I felt like I was where I was meant to be, doing what I was supposed to be doing.

Life, like a poem, is a series of choices.

Something had shifted, maybe just slightly, but perceptibly. I remember feeling the smile on my face the whole walk back to the hotel, hoping it didn't seem odd to the people around me. I stopped at the drawbridge that lifted so the boats could go under. The whole street lifted up right in front of me. Nothing seemed impossible anymore. Everything was possible.

BRIDE

How long have I been wed
to myself? Calling myself

darling, dressing for my own
pleasure, each morning

choosing perfume to turn
me on. How long have I been

alone in this house but not
alone? Married less

to the man than to the woman
silvering with the mirror.

I know the kind of wife
I need and I become her:

the one who will leave
this earth at the same instant

I do. I am my own bride,
lifting the veil to see

my face. Darling, I say,
I have waited for you all my life.

ACKNOWLEDGMENTS

Thank you to my agent, Joy Tutela, and my editor, Julia Cheiffetz. I've said it before and I'll say it again: I'm the luckiest.

Thank you thank you thank you, Megan Stielstra, forever and ever. This book would not exist without you, full stop. Thanks also to Kelly Sundberg and Betsy Crane. The belief the three of you have had in this book—and in me—was contagious. Thank you for making sure I caught it.

Thank you to the whole team at One Signal, Atria, and Simon & Schuster, including Joanna Pinsker, Dayna Johnson, Dana Trocker, Abby Mohr, and Morgan Hoit. What you make happen is extraordinary. Special thanks to Jimmy Iacobelli for the gorgeous cover design.

Thank you, Mom, Dad, Katie, Carly, Travis, and Josh; thank you, Bela; thank you, Kelly; thank you, Jen and Lisa; thank you, Ann, Victoria, Dawn, Saeed, and Wendy; thank you, Gus and Jay; thank you, Dr. Fitch, Dr. Klingensmith, Caroline, Kathryn, Susan, and Megan: you all saved me in ways large and small.

Thank you, Violet and Rhett. You're my why and how and what. You make this place beautiful.

CREDITS

Louise Bourgeois, excerpt from *Louise Bourgeois: Memory and Architecture*. Copyright © 1999 by Louise Bourgeois.

Heather Christle, excerpt from *The Crying Book*. Copyright © 2019 by Heather Christle. Reprinted with the permission of The Permissions Company, LLC on behalf of Catapult Books, www.catapult.co.

John Ciardi, excerpt from *I Marry You*. Copyright © 1958 by John Ciardi. Reprinted with the permission of The Permissions Company, LLC on behalf of Rutgers University Press, www.rutgersuniversitypress.org.

Robert Creeley, excerpt from *Collected Prose: Charles Olson*. Copyright © 1996 by Charles Olson.

Rachel Cusk, excerpt from *Aftermath: On Marriage and Separation*. Copyright © 2012 by Rachel Cusk. Reprinted by permission of Farrar, Straus and Giroux. All Rights Reserved.

John Darnielle, "Picture of My Dress," from *Getting Into Knives* (The Mountain Goats, Merge Records, 2020). Copyright © 2020 by Cadmean Dawn (ASCAP). Used by permission of Pacific Electric Music Publishing.

Emily Dickinson and Mabel Loomis Todd, excerpt from *Letters of Emily Dickinson*. Public Domain.

Joan Didion, excerpt from *Slouching Towards Bethlehem: Essays*. Copyright © 1966, 1968, renewed 1996 by Joan Didion. Reprinted by permission of Farrar, Straus and Giroux. All Rights Reserved.

Linda Gregg, excerpt from *Too Bright to See / Alma: Poems*. Copyright © 2001 by Linda Gregg. Reprinted with the permission of The Permissions Company, LLC on behalf of Graywolf Press, Minneapolis, Minnesota, www.graywolfpress.org.

Zora Neale Hurston, excerpt from *Their Eyes Were Watching God*. Copyright © 1937 by Zora Neale Hurston. Reprinted by permission of Amistad, an imprint of HarperCollins Publishers, New York, New York. All rights reserved.

Clive James, excerpt from *The River in the Sky: A Poem*. Copyright © 2018 by Clive James. Reprinted by permission of W. W. Norton & Company, Inc., New York, New York, www.wwnorton.com.

Audre Lorde, excerpt from *Sister Outsider: Essays and Speeches*. Copyright © 1984 by Audre Lorde. Reprinted with the permission of the Estate of Audre Lorde.

Audre Lorde, excerpt from *The Selected Works of Audre Lorde*. Copyright © 1977 by Audre Lorde. Reprinted by permission of the Estate of Audre Lorde.

Chan Marshall, excerpt from "Woman." Copyright © 2018 Domino Recording Co Ltd. Reprinted by permission of Hal Leonard. All Rights Reserved.

Rhett Miller, excerpt from "The Scraps." Copyright © 2021 by Rhett Miller. Used by permission of Rhett Miller.

Maggie Nelson, excerpt from *Bluets*. Copyright © 2009 by Maggie Nelson. Reprinted by permission of Wave Books, Seattle, Washington, www.wavepoetry.com.

Naomi Shahib Nye, excerpt from "Jerusalem" from Red Suitcase. Copyright © 1994 by Naomi Shihab Nye. Reprinted with the permission of The Permissions Company, LLC on behalf of BOA Editions, Ltd., boaeditions.org.

Lucia Osborne-Crowley, excerpt from *I Choose Elena: On Trauma, Memory and Survival*. Copyright © 2019 by Lucia Osborne-Crowley. Reprinted by permission of The Indigo Press, London, United Kingdom, www.theindigopress.com.

Rainer Maria Rilke, "Geh bis an Deiner Sehnsucht Rand/Go to the Limits of Your Longing" from

ABOUT THE AUTHOR

Maggie Smith is the award-winning author of *Good Bones*, *The Well Speaks of Its Own Poison*, *Lamp of the Body*, and the national bestsellers *Goldenrod* and *Keep Moving: Notes on Loss, Creativity, and Change*. A 2011 recipient of a Creative Writing Fellowship from the National Endowment for the Arts, Smith has also received several Individual Excellence Awards from the Ohio Arts Council, two Academy of American Poets Prizes, a Pushcart Prize, and fellowships from the Sustainable Arts Foundation and the Virginia Center for the Creative Arts. She has been widely published, appearing in the *New York Times*, the *New Yorker*, the *Nation*, the *Paris Review*, the *Best American Poetry*, and more.

@maggiesmithpoet

BOOK
CLUB
FAVORITES
READER'S
GUIDE

You Could
Make This Place
Beautiful

Maggie Smith

This reading group guide for *You Could Make This Place Beautiful* includes an introduction and discussion questions for your book club. The suggested questions are intended to help your reading group find new and interesting angles and topics for your discussion. We hope that these ideas will enrich your conversation and increase your enjoyment of the book.

INTRODUCTION

In her long-awaited debut memoir, *You Could Make This Place Beautiful*, award-winning poet Maggie Smith explores in lyrical vignettes the end of her marriage and the beginning of a surprising new life. A story that starts with Smith's personal, particular heartbreak quickly grows into a reckoning with contemporary womanhood, family, work, and patriarchy. With the spirit of reflection and empathy she's known for, and a razor-sharp wit, Smith interweaves snapshots of a life with meditations on secrets, anger, forgiveness, and narrative itself.

You Could Make This Place Beautiful is an unflinching look at what it means to live and write our own lives. It is a story about a mother's fierce and constant love for her children, and a woman's love and regard for herself. Above all, this memoir is an argument for possibility. With a poet's attention to language and a transformation of the genre, Smith reveals how, in the aftermath of loss, we can discover our power and make something new. Something beautiful.

TOPICS AND QUESTIONS
FOR DISCUSSION

1) *You Could Make This Place Beautiful* plays with the genre of memoir both in terms of style and structure. How was the book different from other memoirs you have read?

2) Smith writes that this book isn't a "tell-all," it's a "tell-mine." Through the course of the book, one has the sense that Smith will never fully understand what happened to her marriage. How do we move forward in life when we experience inexplicable ruptures (a friendship that ends suddenly, the unexpected loss of a job)? How can we make peace with the not knowing?

3) The epigraph of the book is a quote from Emily Dickenson: "I am out with lanterns, looking for myself." In what ways is this memoir a search for self, or even an excavation of self?

4) In "A Note on Setting" on page 13, Smith writes "If you opened me up, you'd find Ohio. . . . Setting is not just *where* I am, it's who I am and what I am and why. It's not just where I live, it's *how* I live." Do you feel this connection to your current home or a past one? What role does it play in your identity and how you live your life?

5) Throughout much of the book, Smith discusses her past and current selves, noting, "We are all nesting dolls, carrying the earlier iterations of ourselves inside. . . . Inside forty-something me is the woman I was in my thirties, the woman I was in my twenties, the teenager I was, the child I was." If you had to think of your own life in this way, what moments stand out? What are the past versions you envision of yourself?

6) How do issues of domestic labor and traditional gender roles play out in the book? Were there aspects of Smith's story that you related to?

7) In reflecting on her marriage and her own mother's life in the family home, Smith notes, "I saw myself and my husband as different—more progressive, more equal in our household, both with graduate degrees, both respected in our fields—but were we? The division of labor in our home told a different story." How do you divide and think about labor in your own home? Do you wish it were different or want to change it? Did Smith's discussion of these themes throughout the book impact your thinking at all?

8) Smith writes, "what would happen if I weren't needed as a caregiver? What would the story be?" What would *your* life look like if you weren't needed as a caregiver? What would be different, both in how you live your daily life and how you perceive yourself?

9) Throughout the book, Smith sets boundaries with the reader, choosing to reveal certain details and omit others, even naming a chapter, "This Moment Isn't for You." What did you think of these narrative choices? Were there times you wanted to know more? Why do you think that is? Are there details you omit when thinking about the story of your own life or when describing it to others?

10) Smith frequently discusses the music that forms the soundtrack of her life. Do you have artists in your life that you feel especially connected to? What role does music play in your daily life and in your memory-making?

11) After Smith's poem "Good Bones" goes viral, she tells a reporter, "I feel like I go into a phone booth and I turn into a poet sometimes. Most of the other time, I'm just Maggie who pushes the stroller." If you're a parent, do you feel this separation in identity between your work and your role as a parent? How does that separation make you feel?

12) The title of the book is taken from the last sentence of Smith's viral poem in which she states, "I am trying / to sell them the world. Any decent realtor, / walking you through a real shithole, chirps on / about good bones: This place could be beautiful, / right? You could make this place beautiful." How do you "make this place beautiful" in difficult times?

13) In "A Note on the Title," Smith writes, "Sometimes I feel like I titled this book *Kittens and Rainbows*, and then I wrote hell." What were your expectations of the book before reading it, based on the title and cover? How did they change or stay the same after reading?

14) On page 110, Smith describes her social-media post that would eventually lead to her book *Keep Moving*. Have you read any of Smith's other poems or essays? How does her previous work connect to and/or differ from *You Could Make This Place Beautiful*?

15) Consider the first sentence of the book (the epigraph, "I am out with lanterns, looking for myself") and the last sentence of the book ("I have waited for you all my life"). Do you think Smith finds herself in the end?